Strengthening Math Skills
Addition and Subtraction

MW00612673

Contents

Introduction

Building a solid foundation in math is a student's key to success in school and in the future. This book will help students to develop basic math skills that they will use every day. As students build on math skills that they already know and learn new math skills, they will see how much math connects to real life.

This book will help students to:

- develop math competency.
- acquire basic math skills and concepts.
- learn a variety of strategies to help them solve number sentences.
- learn problem-solving strategies.
- apply these skills and strategies to everyday life.
- gain confidence in their own ability to succeed at learning.

Students who have self-confidence in their math skills often do better in other school areas, too. Mastering math helps students to become better learners and better students.

Ensure Student Success in Math

This book contains several features that help teachers to build the self-confidence of math students. This book enables the teacher to:

- reach students by providing a unique approach to math content.
- help students build basic foundational math skills.
- provide individualized, differentiated instruction.

Assessment. An assessment is included to serve as a diagnostic tool. The assessment contains many of the math concepts presented in this book. The assessment helps to pinpoint each student's strengths and weaknesses. Then, instruction can be focused on the math content each student needs.

Correlation to Standards. A correlation to NCTM Standards is provided to allow teachers to tailor their teaching to standardized tests. This chart shows teachers at a glance which lessons cover the basic skills students are expected to master.

Glossary. Math has a language of its own, so a glossary of math terms is included at the front of the book.

Lesson Format. Each lesson in the book is constructed to help students to master the specific concept covered in the lesson. A short introduction explains the concept. Then, a step-by-step process is used to work an example problem. Students are then given a short problem to work on their own. Finally, a page of practice problems that reinforce the concept is provided.

Graphic Organizers. Graphic organizers often help students to solve problems more easily. For that reason, manipulatives, workmats, strategy methods, and other helpful blacklines are supplied at the back of the book. Students can use these tools to help them solve the problems in the book or to create their own problems.

Answer Key. An answer key is provided in the back of the book so students or teachers can check the answers.

Working Together to Help Students Achieve

No student wants to do poorly. There are many reasons students may be having problems with math. This book presents a well-organized, straightforward approach to helping students overcome the obstacles that may hold them back. This book and your instruction can help students to regain their footing and continue their climb to math achievement.

A short introduction explains the concept.

An **Example** problem is explained step by step.

On Your Own has students work one problem on their own.

Building Skills provides students with repeated practice of the skill.

Problem Solving allows students to work a word problem that is related to the skill.

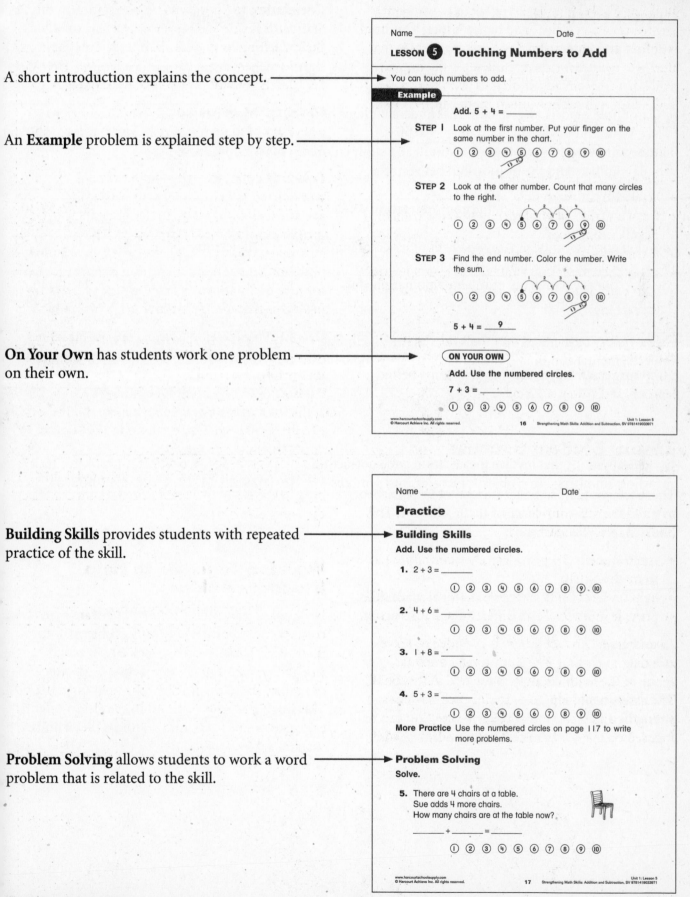

Correlation to NCTM Standards

Content Strands   Lesson

Number and Operation

Content Strands	Lesson
• count with understanding and recognize "how many" in sets of objects	1, 2, 3, 12, 13, 14, 27, 32
• use multiple models to develop initial understandings of place value and the base-ten number system	26, 27, 39, 40
• understand various meanings of addition and subtraction of whole numbers and the relationship between the two operations	25, 34, 38, 45
• understand the effects of adding and subtracting whole numbers	1, 2, 3, 6, 7, 8, 12, 13, 14, 17, 19, 27, 39, 40, 41, 42, 43, 44, 45, 46, 47, 48, 49, 50, 51
• develop and use strategies for whole-number computations, with a focus on addition and subtraction	All lessons
• develop fluency with basic number combinations for addition and subtraction	7, 11, 17, 18, 23, 24, 31, 33, 34, 35, 36, 37, 38, 40, 41, 42, 43, 44, 45, 46, 47, 48, 49, 50, 51
• use a variety of methods and tools to compute, including objects, mental computation, estimation, paper and pencil, and calculators	3, 4, 5, 6, 7, 9, 10, 14, 15, 16, 20, 21, 22, 26, 27, 28, 29, 30, 31, 32, 35, 36, 40

Algebra

Content Strands	Lesson
• model situations that involve the addition and subtraction of whole numbers, using objects, pictures, and symbols	1, 2, 3, 4, 5, 6, 7, 9, 12, 13, 14, 15, 16, 17, 18, 20, 21, 22, 27, 28, 29, 30, 32, 34, 35

Assessment

Solve.

1. $6 + 3 =$ _____

2. $8 - 0 =$ _____

3. $14 - 7 =$ _____

4. $17 - 9 =$ _____

5. $4 + 8 =$ _____

6. $9 + 9 =$ _____

7.
$$\begin{array}{r} 13 \\ + \ 6 \\ \hline \end{array}$$

8.
$$\begin{array}{r} 47 \\ - \ 9 \\ \hline \end{array}$$

9.
$$\begin{array}{r} 38 \\ - 26 \\ \hline \end{array}$$

10.
$$\begin{array}{r} 55 \\ + 36 \\ \hline \end{array}$$

11.
$$\begin{array}{r} 364 \\ - \ 51 \\ \hline \end{array}$$

12.
$$\begin{array}{r} 523 \\ + \ 62 \\ \hline \end{array}$$

13.
$$\begin{array}{r} 341 \\ + 279 \\ \hline \end{array}$$

14.
$$\begin{array}{r} 400 \\ - 208 \\ \hline \end{array}$$

15. Write the number sentences for the fact family 4, 5, 9.

_____ _____

_____ _____

Strengthening Math Skills: Addition and Subtraction, SV 9781419033971

Assessment

Solve.

1. There are 6 birds on a fence.
Then 4 birds fly away.
How many birds are left?

_____

2. Len has 9 fish in his tank.
He buys 3 more fish.
How many fish does Len have in his tank now?

_____

3. Tony's book is 36 pages long.
He has read 18 pages.
How many more pages does Tony have to read?

_____

4. One train car has 47 people.
Another train car has 39 people.
How many people are there altogether?

_____

5. There are 329 cans of peanuts.
There are 221 cans of walnuts.
How many cans of nuts are there in all?

_____

Glossary

add
to join two or more groups

addend
a number added to another number

addition table
a chart that helps find the sum of addends

calculator
a machine that helps find the answers to math problems

check
to use addition to make sure that the difference in a subtraction problem is correct

cube
a manipulative that stands for one item

difference
the answer in a subtraction sentence

equals (=)
the sign that means to solve the problem

even number
a number ending in 2, 4, 6, 8, or 0

fact
an addition or a subtraction sentence where the two numbers range from 0 to 9

fact family
three numbers that are related through addition and subtraction

flat
a manipulative that stands for one hundred items

mental math
solving a problem by thinking

minuend
the largest number in a subtraction sentence

minus sign (−)
the sign that means to subtract numbers

number line
a line showing numbers

odd number
a number ending in 1, 3, 5, 7, or 9

place-value chart
a chart that shows place value to help add or subtract

plus sign (+)
the sign that means to add numbers

regroup
to change ones, tens, or hundreds

rod
a manipulative that stands for ten items

solve
to find the answer

subtract
to take away from a group

subtrahend
the number subtracted from the minuend

sum
the answer in an addition sentence

ten frame
a tool with ten blocks to help form groups of tens and ones

Name _____ Date _____

LESSON ① Joining Groups

You can join two groups.

Write how many pigs in all.

_____   _____ | _____ in all

STEP 1 Count how many are standing. Write the number.

____4____   _____ | _____ in all

STEP 2 Count how many join. Write the number.

____4____   ____1____ | _____ in all

STEP 3 Count how many in all. Write the number.

____4____   ____1____ | ____5____ in all

There are 5 pigs in all.

Name _____ Date _____

Practice

Building Skills

Write how many in all.

1.

_____   _____ | _____ in all

2.

_____   _____ | _____ in all

3.

_____   _____ | _____ in all

Problem Solving

Solve.

4. 4 hens are in a pen.
   2 hens run into the pen.
   How many hens in all?
   _____ hens in all

Unit 1: Lesson 1
Strengthening Math Skills: Addition and Subtraction, SV 9781419033971

LESSON ② Writing Addition Sentences

You add to join groups. You can show how you add. You can write an addition sentence. You will use a **+** sign. You will use an **=** sign, too.

Example

Write the addition sentence.

_____ + _____ = _____

STEP 1 Count how many in the first set. Write the number.

___3___ + _____ = _____

STEP 2 Count how many in the other set. Write the number.

___3___ + ___1___ = _____

STEP 3 Count how many in all. Write the number.

___3___ + ___1___ = ___4___

The addition sentence is 3 + 1 = 4.

ON YOUR OWN

Write the addition sentence.

_____ + _____ = _____

Strengthening Math Skills: Addition and Subtraction, SV 9781419033971

Name _____ Date _____

Practice

Building Skills

Write the addition sentence.

1.

_____ + _____ = _____

2.

_____ + _____ = _____

3.

_____ + _____ = _____

Problem Solving

Solve.

4. 3 are at the zoo.

3 join the zoo.

How many in all?

_____

Name _____ Date _____

LESSON ③ Adding Using Counters

You can use counters to add. The answer is the **sum**.

Example

Add. 3 + 2 = _____

STEP 1   Look at the first number. Put in that many counters.

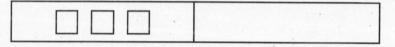

3   +   2 = _____

STEP 2   Look at the other number. Put in that many counters.

3   +   2 = _____

STEP 3   Count how many in all. Write the sum.

3   +   2 = __5__

3 + 2 = 5

(ON YOUR OWN)

Add. Use the counters on page 114.

2 + 4 = _____

Name _____ Date _____

Practice

Building Skills

Add. Use the counters on page 114.

1.

1 + 3 = _____

2.

4 + 2 = _____

3.

2 + 3 = _____

4.

3 + 3 = _____

More Practice Use the addition workmats on page 115 to write more problems.

Problem Solving

Solve.

5. John has 2 fish.
He gets 2 more fish.
How many fish does John have in all?

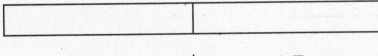

_____ + _____ = _____

Name _____ Date _____

LESSON ④ Adding on a Number Line

You can use a number line to add.

Example

Add. 5 + 2 = _____

STEP 1 Look at the first number. Put a dot above that number on the number line.

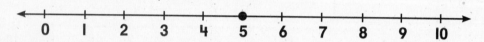

STEP 2 Look at the other number. Move that many places right.

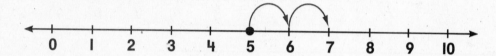

STEP 3 Find the end number. Circle the number. Write the sum.

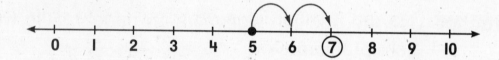

5 + 2 = ___7___

(ON YOUR OWN)

Add. Use the number line.

4 + 4 = _____

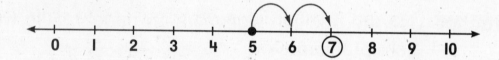

Name _____ Date _____

Practice

Building Skills

Add. Use the number lines.

1. 7 + 2 = _____

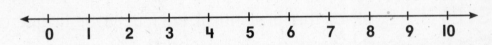

2. 4 + 3 = _____

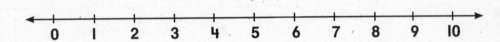

3. 2 + 6 = _____

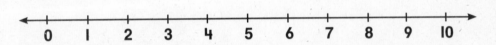

4. 1 + 8 = _____

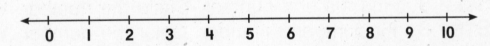

More Practice Use the number lines on page 116 to write more addition sentences.

Problem Solving

Solve.

5. There are 4 children cleaning up the park. Then 2 more children come to help. How many children are cleaning up the park now?

_____ + _____ = _____

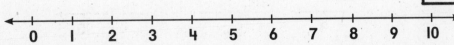

Unit 1: Lesson 4
Strengthening Math Skills: Addition and Subtraction, SV 9781419033971

Name _____ Date _____

LESSON **5** Touching Numbers to Add

You can touch numbers to add.

Example

Add. 5 + 4 = _____

STEP 1 Look at the first number. Put your finger on the same number in the chart.

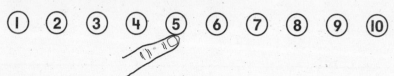

STEP 2 Look at the other number. Count that many circles to the right.

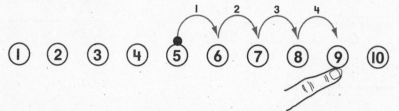

STEP 3 Find the end number. Color the number. Write the sum.

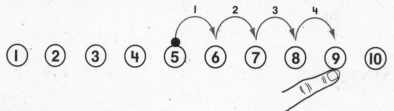

5 + 4 = ____9____

ON YOUR OWN

Add. Use the numbered circles.

7 + 3 = _____

① ② ③ ④ ⑤ ⑥ ⑦ ⑧ ⑨ ⑩

Practice

Building Skills

Add. Use the numbered circles.

1. $2 + 3 =$ _____

① ② ③ ④ ⑤ ⑥ ⑦ ⑧ ⑨ ⑩

2. $4 + 6 =$ _____

① ② ③ ④ ⑤ ⑥ ⑦ ⑧ ⑨ ⑩

3. $1 + 8 =$ _____

① ② ③ ④ ⑤ ⑥ ⑦ ⑧ ⑨ ⑩

4. $5 + 3 =$ _____

① ② ③ ④ ⑤ ⑥ ⑦ ⑧ ⑨ ⑩

More Practice Use the numbered circles on page 117 to write more problems.

Problem Solving

Solve.

5. There are 4 chairs at a table.
Sue adds 4 more chairs.
How many chairs are at the table now?

_____ + _____ = _____

① ② ③ ④ ⑤ ⑥ ⑦ ⑧ ⑨ ⑩

LESSON 6 Order in Addition

Numbers can be added in any order. The sum is the same.

Example

Add. 3 + 2 = _____   2 + 3 = _____

STEP 1 Point to 3 + 2. Look at the first number. Color that many cubes red.

3 + 2 = _____

| R | R | R | | | | | | | |

2 + 3 = _____

| | | | | | | | | | |

STEP 2 Look at the other number. Color that many cubes blue. Add 3 + 2. Write the sum.

3 + 2 = ___5___

| R | R | R | B | B | | | | | |

2 + 3 = _____

| | | | | | | | | | |

STEP 3 Point to 2 + 3. Look at the first number. Color that many cubes red.

3 + 2 = ___5___

| R | R | R | B | B | | | | | |

2 + 3 = _____

| R | R | | | | | | | | |

STEP 4 Look at the other number. Color that many cubes blue. Add 2 + 3. Write the sum.

3 + 2 = ___5___

| R | R | R | B | B | | | | | |

2 + 3 = ___5___

| R | R | B | B | B | | | | | |

3 + 2 = 5 has the same sum as 2 + 3 = 5.

Name _____ Date _____

Add. Color the cubes to show each addition sentence.

6 + 1 = _____   1 + 6 = _____

[| | | | | | | | | |]   [| | | | | | | | | |]

Practice

Building Skills

Add. Color the cubes to show each addition sentence.

1.   3 + 5 = _____   5 + 3 = _____

[| | | | | | | | | |]   [| | | | | | | | | |]

2.   9 + 1 = _____   1 + 9 = _____

[| | | | | | | | | |]   [| | | | | | | | | |]

3.   4 + 3 = _____   3 + 4 = _____

[| | | | | | | | | |]   [| | | | | | | | | |]

4.   2 + 6 = _____   6 + 2 = _____

[| | | | | | | | | |]   [| | | | | | | | | |]

Problem Solving

Write two addition sentences. Then solve.

5. Rosa has 7 blue pens.
She has 2 red pens.
How many pens does Rosa have in all?

_____ + _____ = _____   _____ + _____ = _____

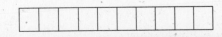

Name _____ Date _____

LESSON **7** **Adding Zero**

When 0 (zero) is added to any number, the sum is that number.

Example

Add. 4 + 0 = _____

STEP 1 Look at the first number. Put in that many counters.

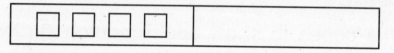

STEP 2 Look at the other number. Put in that many counters.

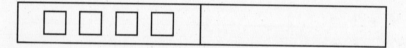

STEP 3 Count how many in all. Write the sum.

4 + 0 = ____4____

4 + 0 = 4

(**ON YOUR OWN**)

Add. Use the counters on page 114.

0 + 6 = _____

Name _____ Date _____

Practice

Building Skills

Add. Use the counters on page 114.

1. ⬜⬜

$$7 \quad + \quad 0 = \underline{\hspace{2cm}}$$

2. ⬜⬜

$$0 \quad + \quad 1 = \underline{\hspace{2cm}}$$

3. ⬜⬜

$$0 \quad + \quad 3 = \underline{\hspace{2cm}}$$

4. ⬜⬜

$$9 \quad + \quad 0 = \underline{\hspace{2cm}}$$

Problem Solving

Solve.

5. Max has 2 green apples.
He has no red apples.
How many apples does Max have in all?

$$\underline{\hspace{1.5cm}} + \underline{\hspace{1.5cm}} = \underline{\hspace{1.5cm}}$$

Name _____ Date _____

LESSON **8** Vertical Adding

Numbers can be added across. Numbers can be added down.
The sum is the same.

Write the addition problems two ways. Then add.

_____ + _____ = _____

_____
+ _____

STEP 1 Look at the boxes that go across. Write the number
sentence. Write the sum.

___2___ + ___3___ = ___5___

_____
+ _____
_____

STEP 2 Look at the boxes that go down. Write the number
for the top box. Write the number for the bottom
box. Write the sum.

___2___ + ___3___ = ___5___

   2
+ 3
   5

Name _____ Date _____

Write the addition problems two ways. Then add.

_____ + _____ = _____

_____
+ _____
_____

Practice

Building Skills

Write the addition problems two ways. Then add.

1.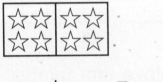

_____ + _____ = _____

_____
+ _____
_____

2.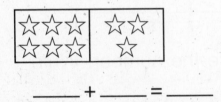

_____ + _____ = _____

_____
+ _____
_____

Problem Solving

Write the addition problems two ways. Then solve.

3. Kim saw 3 stars in the sky.
   Then she saw 4 stars in the sky.
   How many stars did Kim see altogether?

_____ + _____ = _____

_____
+ _____
_____

Strengthening Math Skills: Addition and Subtraction, SV 9781419033971

Unit 1: Lesson 8

Name _____ Date _____

LESSON 9 Counting On

You can find sums by counting on. Look for the numbers 1, 2, or 3.

Example

Add. 2 + 6 = _____

STEP 1 Look for a number that is 1, 2, or 3. Then you can count on.

2 + 6 = _____

Think
There is a 2.

STEP 2 Find the larger number. Put a dot over the same number on the number line.

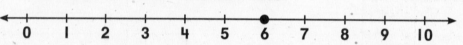

STEP 3 Look at the smaller number. Move that many places right.

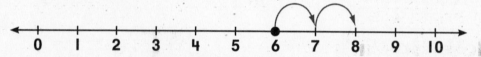

STEP 4 Find the end number. Circle the number. Write the sum.

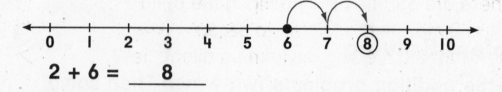

2 + 6 = _____8_____

ON YOUR OWN

Add by counting on.

8 + 1 = _____

Name _____ Date _____

Practice

Building Skills

Add by counting on.

1. $4 + 3 =$ _____

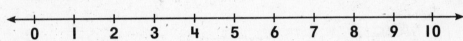

2. $1 + 6 =$ _____

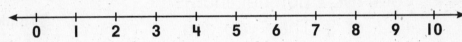

3. $8 + 2 =$ _____

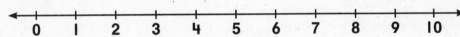

4. $1 + 7 =$ _____

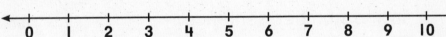

More Practice Use the number lines on page 116 to write more counting on addition sentences.

Problem Solving

Solve.

5. There are 6 turtles swimming in the pond.
Then 3 more turtles come to swim.
How many turtles are swimming altogether?

_____ + _____ = _____

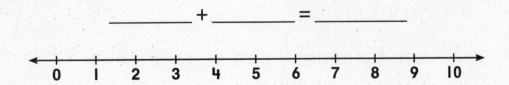

Name _____ Date _____

LESSON 10 Counting On Using Mental Math

You can count on in your mind. Look for the numbers 1, 2, or 3 in the number sentence.

Example

Add. 5 + 3 = _____

STEP 1 Look for a number that is 1, 2, or 3. Then you can count on.

5 + 3 = _____

Think
There is a 3.

STEP 2 Find the larger number in the number sentence. Think about that number in your mind.

Think 5.

STEP 3 Look at the smaller number. Count on that many more in your mind. Write the sum.

5 + 3 = ___8___

Think 5, 6, 7, 8.

ON YOUR OWN

Add by counting on in your mind.

2 + 4 = _____

Think _____
_____

26   Strengthening Math Skills: Addition and Subtraction, SV 9781419033971

Name _____ Date _____

Practice

Building Skills

Add by counting on in your mind.

1. 6 + 1 = _____

2. 3 + 7 = _____

3. 1 + 9 = _____

4. 6 + 2 = _____

Problem Solving

Solve.

5. Jaida had 5 balloons.
She blew up 2 more.
How many balloons did Jaida have in all?

_____ + _____ = _____

Name _____ Date _____

LESSON 11 Adding Facts to 10

Addition problems that have a sum of 10 or less are called **facts**.
You should know these facts very well.

Example

Here are some facts with 4. Add. Write the sums as quickly as you can.

4	4	0	4	1	6	4
+ 2	+ 4	+ 4	+ 5	+ 4	+ 4	+ 3

STEP 1 Tap your pencil on the table.

STEP 2 Quickly write the sum for 4 + 2 above.

STEP 3 Tap your pencil on the table again.

STEP 4 Quickly write the sum for 4 + 4 above.

STEP 5 Repeat the steps of tapping and writing a sum very quickly to answer the other problems.

STEP 6 Use the addition table on page 118 to check your sums.

(**ON YOUR OWN**)

Add. Write the sums as quickly as you can.

6	2	3	5	8	1	2
+ 1	+ 7	+ 3	+ 0	+ 2	+ 9	+ 4

Name _____   Date _____

Practice

Building Skills

Add. Write the sums as quickly as you can.

1.
$$\begin{array}{r} 4 \\ +3 \\ \hline \end{array} \quad \begin{array}{r} 2 \\ +5 \\ \hline \end{array} \quad \begin{array}{r} 8 \\ +0 \\ \hline \end{array} \quad \begin{array}{r} 1 \\ +5 \\ \hline \end{array} \quad \begin{array}{r} 6 \\ +3 \\ \hline \end{array} \quad \begin{array}{r} 5 \\ +5 \\ \hline \end{array} \quad \begin{array}{r} 1 \\ +8 \\ \hline \end{array}$$

2.
$$\begin{array}{r} 6 \\ +2 \\ \hline \end{array} \quad \begin{array}{r} 7 \\ +3 \\ \hline \end{array} \quad \begin{array}{r} 9 \\ +1 \\ \hline \end{array} \quad \begin{array}{r} 0 \\ +0 \\ \hline \end{array} \quad \begin{array}{r} 2 \\ +3 \\ \hline \end{array} \quad \begin{array}{r} 1 \\ +5 \\ \hline \end{array} \quad \begin{array}{r} 3 \\ +3 \\ \hline \end{array}$$

3.
$$\begin{array}{r} 2 \\ +7 \\ \hline \end{array} \quad \begin{array}{r} 0 \\ +6 \\ \hline \end{array} \quad \begin{array}{r} 3 \\ +5 \\ \hline \end{array} \quad \begin{array}{r} 5 \\ +2 \\ \hline \end{array} \quad \begin{array}{r} 1 \\ +9 \\ \hline \end{array} \quad \begin{array}{r} 3 \\ +7 \\ \hline \end{array} \quad \begin{array}{r} 5 \\ +4 \\ \hline \end{array}$$

4.
$$\begin{array}{r} 2 \\ +2 \\ \hline \end{array} \quad \begin{array}{r} 3 \\ +0 \\ \hline \end{array} \quad \begin{array}{r} 1 \\ +3 \\ \hline \end{array} \quad \begin{array}{r} 5 \\ +3 \\ \hline \end{array} \quad \begin{array}{r} 0 \\ +8 \\ \hline \end{array} \quad \begin{array}{r} 4 \\ +6 \\ \hline \end{array} \quad \begin{array}{r} 2 \\ +8 \\ \hline \end{array}$$

Problem Solving

Solve.

5. There are 3 flowers in a vase.
Keisha puts 6 more flowers in the vase.
How many flowers are in the vase now?

_____ + _____ = _____

Strengthening Math Skills: Addition and Subtraction, SV 9781419033971

LESSON ⓬ Taking Away from a Group

You can take away from a group.

Write how many birds are left.

_____   _____ | _____ are left.

STEP 1 Count how many in all. Write the number.

__3___   _____ | _____ are left.

STEP 2 Count how many go away. Write the number.

__3___   __1___ | _____ are left.

STEP 3 Count how many are left. Write the number.

__3___   __1___ | __2___ are left.

There are 2 birds left.

(**ON YOUR OWN**)

Write how many rabbits are left.

_____   _____ | _____ are left.

Practice

Building Skills

Write how many are left.

1.

_____ _____ | _____ are left.

2.

 |

_____ _____ | _____ are left.

3.

 |

_____ _____ | _____ are left.

Problem Solving

Solve.

4. There are 4 bugs on a leaf.
Then 1 bug flies away.
How many bugs are left?

 |

_____ bugs are left.

LESSON ⑬ Writing Subtraction Sentences

When you take away from a group, you subtract. You can show how you subtract. You can write a subtraction sentence. You will use a – sign. You will use an = sign, too.

Example

Write the subtraction sentence.

_____ – _____ = _____

STEP 1 Count how many in all.
Write the number.

_____6_____ – _____ = _____

STEP 2 Count how many go away.
Write the number.

_____6_____ – _____3_____ = _____

STEP 3 Count how many are left.
Write the number.

_____6_____ – _____3_____ = _____3_____

The subtraction sentence is 6 – 3 = 3.

(**ON YOUR OWN**)

Write the subtraction sentence.

_____ – _____ = _____

Name _____ Date _____

Practice

Building Skills

Write the subtraction sentences.

1.

_____ – _____ = _____

2.

_____ – _____ = _____

3.

_____ – _____ = _____

Problem Solving

Solve.

4. 5 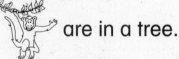 are in a tree.

3 climb out of the tree.

How many are left?

_____

Unit 1: Lesson 13
Strengthening Math Skills: Addition and Subtraction, SV 9781419033971

Name _____ Date _____

LESSON ⑭ Subtracting Using Counters

You can use counters to subtract. The answer is the **difference**.

Example

Subtract. 6 – 3 = _____

STEP 1 Look at the first number. Put in that many counters.

6 – 3 = _____

STEP 2 Look at the other number. Take away that many counters.

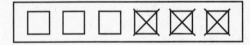

6 – 3 = _____

STEP 3 Count how many are left. Write the difference.

6 – 3 = ___3___

6 – 3 = 3

(ON YOUR OWN)

Subtract. Use the counters on page 114.

5 – 4 = _____

[_____]

Name _____ Date _____

Practice

Building Skills

Subtract. Use the counters on page 114.

1.

┌─────────────────────────────┐
│   │
└─────────────────────────────┘

3 – 2 = _____

2.

┌─────────────────────────────┐
│   │
└─────────────────────────────┘

5 – 3 = _____

3.

┌─────────────────────────────┐
│   │
└─────────────────────────────┘

4 – 2 = _____

4.

┌─────────────────────────────┐
│   │
└─────────────────────────────┘

2 – 1 = _____

More Practice Use the subtraction workmats on page 119 to write more problems.

Problem Solving

Solve.

5. There are 5 nuts in a tree.
A squirrel takes 1 nut.
How many nuts are left in the tree?

┌─────────────────────────────┐
│   │
└─────────────────────────────┘

_____ – _____ = _____

Strengthening Math Skills: Addition and Subtraction, SV 9781419033971

Name _____ Date _____

LESSON ⓯ Subtracting on a Number Line

You can use a number line to subtract.

Example

Subtract. 8 – 3 = _____

STEP 1 Look at the first number. Put a dot above that number on the number line.

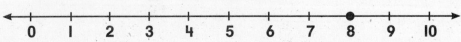

STEP 2 Look at the other number. Move that many places left.

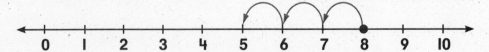

STEP 3 Find the end number. Circle the number. Write the difference.

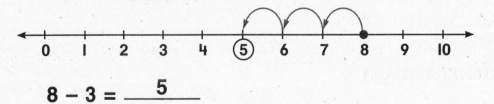

8 – 3 = __5__

(**ON YOUR OWN**)

Subtract. Use the number line.

6 – 2 = _____

$$\overleftrightarrow{\quad 0 \quad 1 \quad 2 \quad 3 \quad 4 \quad 5 \quad 6 \quad 7 \quad 8 \quad 9 \quad 10 \quad}$$

Name _____ Date _____

Practice

Building Skills

Subtract. Use the number lines.

1. $7 - 5 =$ _____

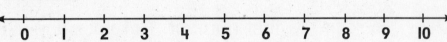

2. $9 - 2 =$ _____

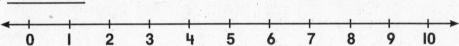

3. $6 - 4 =$ _____

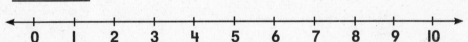

4. $8 - 3 =$ _____

More Practice Use the number lines on page 116 to write more subtraction sentences.

Problem Solving

Solve.

5. There are 7 bees near a hive.
Then 3 bees fly away.
How many bees are left?

_____ − _____ = _____

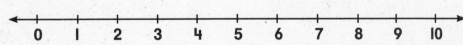

Unit 1: Lesson 15
Strengthening Math Skills: Addition and Subtraction, SV 9781419033971

Name _____ Date _____

LESSON 16   Touching Numbers to Subtract

You can touch numbers to subtract.

Example

Subtract. 9 − 3 = _____

STEP 1   Look at the first number. Put your finger on the same number in the chart.

STEP 2   Look at the other number. Count that many circles to the left.

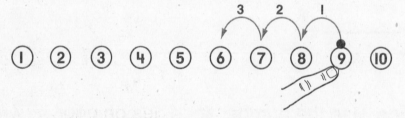

STEP 3   Find the end number. Color the number. Write the difference.

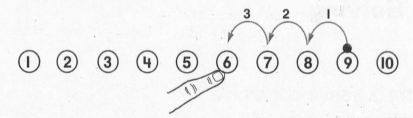

9 − 3 = ___6___

(**ON YOUR OWN**)

Subtract. Use the numbered circles.

7 − 2 = _____

① ② ③ ④ ⑤ ⑥ ⑦ ⑧ ⑨ ⑩

Practice

Building Skills

Subtract. Use the numbered circles.

1. $8 - 5 =$ _____

①　②　③　④　⑤　⑥　⑦　⑧　⑨　⑩

2. $7 - 5 =$ _____

①　②　③　④　⑤　⑥　⑦　⑧　⑨　⑩

3. $3 - 2 =$ _____

①　②　③　④　⑤　⑥　⑦　⑧　⑨　⑩

4. $9 - 4 =$ _____

①　②　③　④　⑤　⑥　⑦　⑧　⑨　⑩

More Practice Use the numbered circles on page 117 to write more problems.

Problem Solving

Solve.

5. Mrs. Ling buys 6 oranges.
Her family eats 4 oranges.
How many oranges are left?

_____ – _____ = _____

①　②　③　④　⑤　⑥　⑦　⑧　⑨　⑩

Name _____ Date _____

LESSON 17 Subtracting Sames

When you subtract a number from the same number, the difference is 0.

Example

Subtract. $8 - 8 =$ _____

STEP 1 Look at the first number. Put in that many counters.

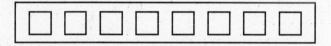

STEP 2 Look at the other number. Take away that many counters.

STEP 3 Count how many are left. Write the difference.

$8 - 8 =$ ___0___

$8 - 8 = 0$

(ON YOUR OWN)

Subtract. Use the counters on page 114.

$4 - 4 =$ _____

Name _____ Date _____

Practice

Building Skills

Subtract. Use the counters on page 114.

1.
┌─────────────────────────────┐
│   │
│   │
└─────────────────────────────┘

$9 - 9 =$ _____

2.
┌─────────────────────────────┐
│   │
│   │
└─────────────────────────────┘

$1 - 1 =$ _____

3.
┌─────────────────────────────┐
│   │
│   │
└─────────────────────────────┘

$3 - 3 =$ _____

4.
┌─────────────────────────────┐
│   │
│   │
└─────────────────────────────┘

$7 - 7 =$ _____

Problem Solving

Solve.

5. Juan has 5 pencils.
   He gives 5 pencils to his friends.
   How many pencils does Juan have left?

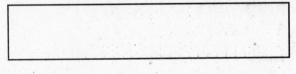

┌─────────────────────────────┐
│   │
│   │
└─────────────────────────────┘

_____ − _____ = _____

Name _____ Date _____

LESSON 18 Subtracting Zero

When you subtract 0 (zero) from any number, the difference is that number.

Example

Subtract. 9 – 0 = _____

STEP 1 Look at the first number. Put in that many counters.

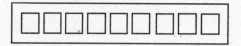

STEP 2 Look at the other number. Take away that many counters.

STEP 3 Count how many are left. Write the difference.

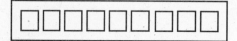

9 – 0 = ___9___

(**ON YOUR OWN**)

Subtract. Use the counters on page 114.

2 – 0 = _____

```

```

Name _____ Date _____

Practice

Building Skills

Subtract. Use the counters on page 114.

1.

┌─────────────────────────┐
│   │
│   │
└─────────────────────────┘

$1 - 0 =$ _____

2.

┌─────────────────────────┐
│   │
│   │
└─────────────────────────┘

$6 - 0 =$ _____

3.

┌─────────────────────────┐
│   │
│   │
└─────────────────────────┘

$4 - 0 =$ _____

4.

┌─────────────────────────┐
│   │
│   │
└─────────────────────────┘

$8 - 0 =$ _____

Problem Solving

Solve.

5. There are 9 people on a bus.
No one gets off at the first stop.
How many people are still on the bus?

┌─────────────────────────┐
│   │
│   │
└─────────────────────────┘

_____ – _____ = _____

43   Strengthening Math Skills: Addition and Subtraction, SV 9781419033971

Unit 1: Lesson 18

Name _____ Date _____

LESSON 19 Vertical Subtracting

Numbers can be subtracted across. Numbers can be subtracted down. The difference is the same.

Example

Write the subtraction problems two ways. Then subtract.

_____ – _____ = _____

_____
– _____
_____

STEP 1 Write the number sentence that goes across. Write the difference.

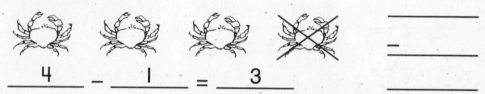

___4___ – ___1___ = ___3___

_____
– _____
_____

STEP 2 Count how many crabs in all. Write the number on the top line. Write how many crabs swim away. Write the number on the middle line.

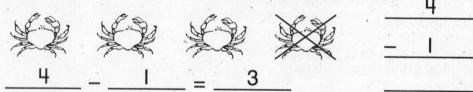

___4___ – ___1___ = ___3___

___4___
– ___1___
_____

STEP 3 Count how many crabs are left. Write the difference on the bottom line.

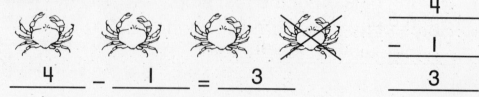

___4___ – ___1___ = ___3___

___4___
– ___1___
___3___

Strengthening Math Skills: Addition and Subtraction, SV 9781419033971

Unit 1: Lesson 19

⬭ ON YOUR OWN

Write the subtraction problems two ways. Then subtract.

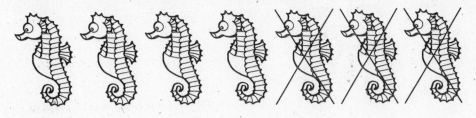

_____ – _____ = _____   _____
                                 –_____

Practice

Building Skills

Write the subtraction problems two ways. Then subtract.

1. ⬭ ⬭ ⬭ ⬭ ⬭ ⬭ ⬭ ⬭   _____
                                –_____
_____ – _____ = _____   _____

2. ⭐ ⭐ ⭐ ⭐ ⭐ ⭐   _____
                                –_____
_____ – _____ = _____   _____

Problem Solving

Write the subtraction sentence two ways. Then solve.

3. Ellen sees 8 fish in the water.
   Then 6 of the fish swim away.
   How many fish are left?

                                              _____
                                             –_____
_____ – _____ = _____   _____

Name _____ Date _____

LESSON 20 Counting Back

You can find differences by counting back. Look for the numbers 1, 2, or 3.

Example

Subtract. 9 − 3 = _____

STEP 1 Look for a number that is 1, 2, or 3. Then you can count back.

9 − 3 = _____

Think
There is a 3.

STEP 2 Find the first number. Put a dot over the same number on the number line.

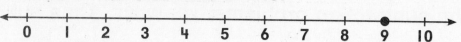

STEP 3 Look at the other number. Move that many places left.

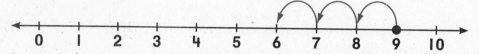

STEP 4 Find the end number. Circle the number. Write the difference.

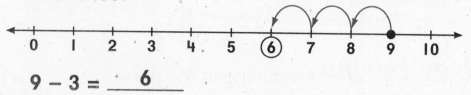

9 − 3 = ___6___

(**ON YOUR OWN**)

Subtract by counting back.

7 − 3 = _____

Strengthening Math Skills: Addition and Subtraction, SV 9781419033971

Unit 1: Lesson 20

Practice

Building Skills

Subtract by counting back.

1. $5 - 3 =$ _____

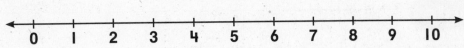

2. $7 - 2 =$ _____

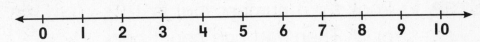

3. $5 - 1 =$ _____

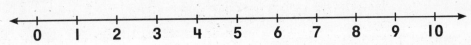

4. $8 - 1 =$ _____

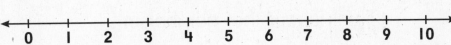

More Practice Use the number lines on page 116 to write more counting back subtraction sentences.

Problem Solving

Solve.

5. There are 9 turtles swimming in the pond.
Then 2 turtles swim away.
How many turtles are left?

_____ – _____ = _____

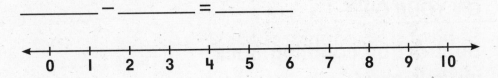

Name _____ Date _____

LESSON 21

Counting Back Using Mental Math

You can count back in your mind. Look for the numbers 1, 2, or 3 in the number sentence.

Example

Subtract. 9 – 2 = _____

STEP 1 Look for a number that is 1, 2, or 3. Then you can count back.

9 – 2 = _____

Think
There is a 2.

STEP 2 Find the larger number. Think about that number in your mind.

Think 9.

STEP 3 Look at the smaller number. Count back that many in your mind. Write the difference.

9 – 2 = ___7___

Think 9, 8, 7.

ON YOUR OWN

Subtract by counting back in your mind.

8 – 3 = _____

Think _____

Strengthening Math Skills: Addition and Subtraction, SV 9781419033971

Practice

Building Skills

Subtract by counting back in your mind.

1. $5 - 2 =$ _____

2. $7 - 1 =$ _____

3. $9 - 3 =$ _____

Problem Solving

Solve.

4. Latoya saw 8 clowns in a car.
2 of the clowns got out.
How many clowns were still in the car?

_____ + _____ = _____

Unit 1: Lesson 21
Strengthening Math Skills: Addition and Subtraction, SV 9781419033971

LESSON 22 Subtracting by Counting Up

You can use a number line to subtract by counting up.

Example

Subtract. 6 − 2 = _____

STEP 1 Look at the smaller number. Put a dot above that number on the number line.

6 − 2 = _____

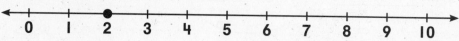

STEP 2 Look at the other number. Circle that number on the number line.

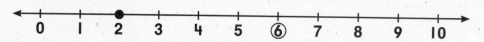

STEP 3 Move right. Count the numbers from the dot to the circled number. Write the difference.

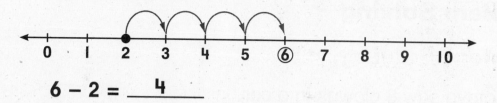

6 − 2 = ___4___

ON YOUR OWN

Subtract by counting up.

8 − 4 = _____

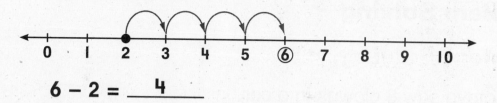

Strengthening Math Skills: Addition and Subtraction, SV 9781419033971

Unit 1: Lesson 22

Name _____ Date _____

Practice

Building Skills

Subtract by counting up.

1. 6 − 3 = _____

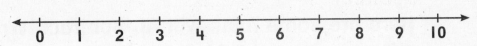

2. 8 − 7 = _____

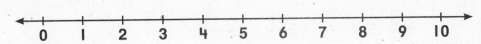

3. 6 − 2 = _____

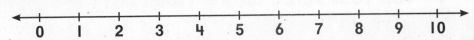

4. 7 − 5 = _____

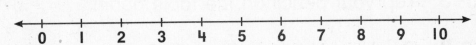

More Practice Use the number lines on page 116 to write more subtraction sentences.

Problem Solving

Solve.

5. Marc has 5 baseball cards. He sells 3 of the cards. How many baseball cards does Marc have left?

_____ − _____ = _____

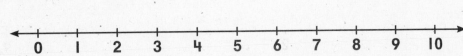

Name _____ Date _____

LESSON 23 Subtracting Facts from 10

Subtraction problems in which the largest number is 10 or less are called **facts.** You should know these facts very well.

Example

Here are some facts with 8. Subtract. Write the differences as quickly as you can.

8	8	8	8	8	8	8	8
-3	-7	-1	-0	-5	-4	-2	-6

STEP 1 Tap your pencil on the table.

STEP 2 Quickly write the difference for 8 − 3 above.

STEP 3 Tap your pencil on the table again.

STEP 4 Quickly write the difference for 8 − 7 above.

STEP 5 Repeat the steps of tapping and writing a difference very quickly to answer the other problems.

ON YOUR OWN

Subtract. Write the differences as quickly as you can.

6	7	4	10	5	9	3
-3	-2	-1	-6	-5	-7	-0

Strengthening Math Skills: Addition and Subtraction, SV 9781419033971

Unit 1: Lesson 23

Practice

Building Skills

Subtract. Write the differences as quickly as you can.

1.
$$\begin{array}{r} 9 \\ -6 \\ \hline \end{array}$$
$$\begin{array}{r} 5 \\ -3 \\ \hline \end{array}$$
$$\begin{array}{r} 4 \\ -2 \\ \hline \end{array}$$
$$\begin{array}{r} 10 \\ -8 \\ \hline \end{array}$$
$$\begin{array}{r} 7 \\ -6 \\ \hline \end{array}$$
$$\begin{array}{r} 6 \\ -3 \\ \hline \end{array}$$
$$\begin{array}{r} 1 \\ -0 \\ \hline \end{array}$$

2.
$$\begin{array}{r} 9 \\ -7 \\ \hline \end{array}$$
$$\begin{array}{r} 10 \\ -7 \\ \hline \end{array}$$
$$\begin{array}{r} 6 \\ -5 \\ \hline \end{array}$$
$$\begin{array}{r} 9 \\ -8 \\ \hline \end{array}$$
$$\begin{array}{r} 8 \\ -6 \\ \hline \end{array}$$
$$\begin{array}{r} 8 \\ -8 \\ \hline \end{array}$$
$$\begin{array}{r} 7 \\ -3 \\ \hline \end{array}$$

3.
$$\begin{array}{r} 4 \\ -2 \\ \hline \end{array}$$
$$\begin{array}{r} 6 \\ -1 \\ \hline \end{array}$$
$$\begin{array}{r} 7 \\ -5 \\ \hline \end{array}$$
$$\begin{array}{r} 8 \\ -0 \\ \hline \end{array}$$
$$\begin{array}{r} 10 \\ -5 \\ \hline \end{array}$$
$$\begin{array}{r} 3 \\ -2 \\ \hline \end{array}$$
$$\begin{array}{r} 5 \\ -2 \\ \hline \end{array}$$

4.
$$\begin{array}{r} 10 \\ -2 \\ \hline \end{array}$$
$$\begin{array}{r} 9 \\ -4 \\ \hline \end{array}$$
$$\begin{array}{r} 4 \\ -3 \\ \hline \end{array}$$
$$\begin{array}{r} 8 \\ -5 \\ \hline \end{array}$$
$$\begin{array}{r} 7 \\ -2 \\ \hline \end{array}$$
$$\begin{array}{r} 3 \\ -0 \\ \hline \end{array}$$
$$\begin{array}{r} 10 \\ -6 \\ \hline \end{array}$$

Problem Solving

Solve.

5. Lena planted 10 flower seeds.
Only 7 of the seeds grew.
How many seeds did not grow?

_____ - _____ = _____

Unit 1: Lesson 23
Strengthening Math Skills: Addition and Subtraction, SV 9781419033971

Name _____ Date _____

LESSON 24 Mixed Operations

Many times there will be both addition and subtraction problems on a page. Look at the sign in each problem. The **+** sign means to add. The **−** sign means to subtract. Then find the sum or difference.

Example

Add or subtract.

10	6	2	8
− 3	+ 2	+ 7	− 2

STEP 1 Look at the sign in the first problem. It means to subtract. Write the difference.

STEP 2 Look at the sign in the next problem. It means to add. Write the sum.

STEP 3 Repeat the steps. Look at each sign. Add or subtract. Write the sums or differences.

10	6	2	8
− 3	+ 2	+ 7	− 2
7	8	9	6

ON YOUR OWN

Add or subtract.

7	8	5	3
+ 3	− 2	− 1	+ 6

Strengthening Math Skills: Addition and Subtraction, SV 9781419033971

Name _____ Date _____

Practice

Building Skills

Add or subtract.

1.
$$\begin{array}{r} 3 \\ +6 \\ \hline \end{array} \qquad \begin{array}{r} 5 \\ -3 \\ \hline \end{array} \qquad \begin{array}{r} 6 \\ -2 \\ \hline \end{array} \qquad \begin{array}{r} 2 \\ +8 \\ \hline \end{array} \qquad \begin{array}{r} 7 \\ +3 \\ \hline \end{array} \qquad \begin{array}{r} 10 \\ -3 \\ \hline \end{array} \qquad \begin{array}{r} 4 \\ +0 \\ \hline \end{array}$$

2.
$$\begin{array}{r} 9 \\ -7 \\ \hline \end{array} \qquad \begin{array}{r} 2 \\ +6 \\ \hline \end{array} \qquad \begin{array}{r} 8 \\ -5 \\ \hline \end{array} \qquad \begin{array}{r} 9 \\ +1 \\ \hline \end{array} \qquad \begin{array}{r} 7 \\ -7 \\ \hline \end{array} \qquad \begin{array}{r} 8 \\ +0 \\ \hline \end{array} \qquad \begin{array}{r} 3 \\ -1 \\ \hline \end{array}$$

3.
$$\begin{array}{r} 6 \\ +4 \\ \hline \end{array} \qquad \begin{array}{r} 7 \\ +1 \\ \hline \end{array} \qquad \begin{array}{r} 9 \\ -5 \\ \hline \end{array} \qquad \begin{array}{r} 8 \\ -2 \\ \hline \end{array} \qquad \begin{array}{r} 2 \\ +2 \\ \hline \end{array} \qquad \begin{array}{r} 5 \\ -4 \\ \hline \end{array} \qquad \begin{array}{r} 4 \\ +3 \\ \hline \end{array}$$

4.
$$\begin{array}{r} 9 \\ -6 \\ \hline \end{array} \qquad \begin{array}{r} 10 \\ -4 \\ \hline \end{array} \qquad \begin{array}{r} 5 \\ +3 \\ \hline \end{array} \qquad \begin{array}{r} 4 \\ +5 \\ \hline \end{array} \qquad \begin{array}{r} 7 \\ -0 \\ \hline \end{array} \qquad \begin{array}{r} 3 \\ +1 \\ \hline \end{array} \qquad \begin{array}{r} 6 \\ -5 \\ \hline \end{array}$$

Problem Solving

Solve.

5. Sal had 8 crackers.
   He put peanut butter on 4 of the crackers.
   He put a slice of cheese on the other crackers.
   How many crackers had cheese?

_____

Name _____ Date _____

LESSON 25 Fact Families

Three numbers are in a fact family. The numbers make two addition sentences. They also make two subtraction sentences.

Example

Write the number sentences for the fact family 4, 3, 7.

STEP 1 Write two addition sentences with the numbers.

$$4 + 3 = 7$$
$$3 + 4 = 7$$

STEP 2 Write two subtraction sentences with the numbers.

$$7 - 4 = 3$$
$$7 - 3 = 4$$

ON YOUR OWN

Write the number sentences for the fact family 6, 2, 8.

_____ + _____ = _____   _____ − _____ = _____

_____ + _____ = _____   _____ − _____ = _____

Name _____ Date _____

Practice

Building Skills

Write the number sentences for each fact family.

1. 4, 1, 5

_____ + _____ = _____   _____ – _____ = _____

_____ + _____ = _____   _____ – _____ = _____

2. 8, 2, 10

_____ + _____ = _____   _____ – _____ = _____

_____ + _____ = _____   _____ – _____ = _____

3. 3, 4, 7

_____ + _____ = _____   _____ – _____ = _____

_____ + _____ = _____   _____ – _____ = _____

4. 6, 3, 9

_____ + _____ = _____   _____ – _____ = _____

_____ + _____ = _____   _____ – _____ = _____

Problem Solving

Solve.

5. Jason had cards with 8, 7, and 1.   [8] [7] [1]
    He wrote number sentences for the fact family using these cards.
    What sentences did Jason write?

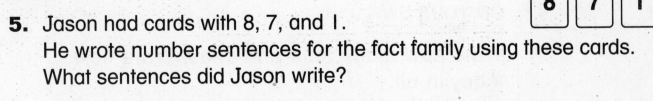

_____ + _____ = _____   _____ – _____ = _____

_____ + _____ = _____   _____ – _____ = _____

Name _____ Date _____

LESSON 26 Tens and Ones

When numbers are greater than 10, look for how many tens and ones.

Write how many tens and ones. Write how many in all.

⬜⬜⬜⬜⬜ _____ ten _____ ones
⬜⬜⬜⬜⬜ _____ in all

STEP 1 Circle a group of ten. Count how many groups of ten. Write how many tens.

⬜⬜⬜⬜⬜⬜ ___1___ ten _____ ones
⬜⬜⬜⬜⬜⬜ _____ in all

STEP 2 Count how many ones. Write how many ones.

⬜⬜⬜⬜⬜⬜ ___1___ ten ___2___ ones
⬜⬜⬜⬜⬜⬜ _____ in all

STEP 3 Write how many in all.

⬜⬜⬜⬜⬜⬜ ___1___ ten ___2___ ones
⬜⬜⬜⬜⬜⬜ __12__ in all

ON YOUR OWN

Write how many tens and ones. Write how many in all.

⬜⬜⬜⬜⬜⬜⬜ _____ ten _____ ones
⬜⬜⬜⬜⬜⬜ _____ in all

Name _____ Date _____

Practice

Building Skills

Write how many tens and ones. Write how many in all.

1. ☐☐☐☐☐☐
   ☐☐☐☐☐   _____ ten _____ one
                 _____ in all

2. ☐☐☐☐☐☐☐☐
   ☐☐☐☐☐☐☐   _____ ten _____ ones
                 _____ in all

3. ☐☐☐☐☐☐☐☐☐
   ☐☐☐☐☐☐☐☐☐   _____ ten _____ ones
                 _____ in all

4. ☐☐☐☐☐☐☐
   ☐☐☐☐☐☐   _____ ten _____ ones
                 _____ in all

Problem Solving

Solve. Draw a picture if you need to.

5. Carlos had 10 marbles in one bag.
   He had 6 marbles in another bag.
   How many marbles did he have in all?

```




```

_____ ten _____ ones
_____ in all

Name _____ Date _____

LESSON **27** Make a Ten

You can make a ten to help you find sums.

Example

Add.   8
      + 6

STEP 1 Look at the first number. Get that many counters. Put the counters in the ten frame.

8
+ 6

STEP 2 Look at the other number. Get that many counters. Put the counters in the frame to fill it. Lay the other counters beside the frame.

8
+ 6

STEP 3 Count the counters outside the frame. Think how many tens and ones. Write the sum.

8
+ 6
‾‾
14

Think I ten and 4 ones

(**ON YOUR OWN**)

Add. Use a ten frame. Use the counters on page 114.

9
+ 7

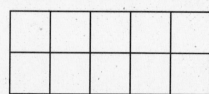

Strengthening Math Skills: Addition and Subtraction, SV 9781419033971

Unit 2: Lesson 27

Name _____ Date _____

Practice

Building Skills

Add. Use a ten frame. Use the counters on page 114.

1. 9
    + 6

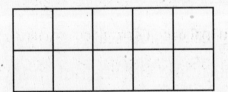

2. 4
    + 8

3. 7
    + 7

Problem Solving

Solve.

4. There were 8 books on one shelf and 5 books on another shelf.
   How many books were there altogether?

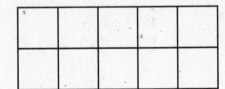

_____

Unit 2: Lesson 27
Strengthening Math Skills: Addition and Subtraction, SV 9781419033971

Name _____ Date _____

LESSON 28 Adding Doubles

When you add two numbers that are the same, you are adding doubles. The sum is always an **even** number. An even number is any number that ends in 2, 4, 6, 8, or 0.

Example

Add. 6 + 6 = _____

STEP 1   Look for numbers that are the same.

STEP 2   Look at the first number. Put in that many counters.

☐ ☐ ☐ ☐ ☐ ☐ |

6 + 6 = _____

STEP 3   Look at the other number. Put in that many counters.

☐ ☐ ☐ ☐ ☐ ☐ | ☐ ☐ ☐ ☐ ☐ ☐

6 + 6 = _____

STEP 4   Count how many in all. Write the sum.

☐ ☐ ☐ ☐ ☐ ☐ | ☐ ☐ ☐ ☐ ☐ ☐

6 + 6 = __12__

6 + 6 = 12

ON YOUR OWN

Add using doubles. Use the counters on page 114.

9 + 9 = _____

Unit 2: Lesson 28
Strengthening Math Skills: Addition and Subtraction, SV 9781419033971

Name _____ Date _____

Practice

Building Skills

Add using doubles. Use the counters on page 114.

1.

3 + 3 = _____

2.

7 + 7 = _____

3.

5 + 5 = _____

Problem Solving

Solve.

4. The Sharks soccer team scored 4 goals
in the first half. The team scored
the same number in the second half.
How many goals did the Sharks score in all?

_____

Strengthening Math Skills: Addition and Subtraction, SV 9781419033971

Name _____ Date _____

LESSON ㉙ Adding Doubles Plus One

When you add two numbers that are one number apart, you are adding doubles plus one. The sum is always an **odd** number in a doubles plus one fact. An odd number ends in 1, 3, 5, 7, or 9.

Example

Add. 5 + 6 = _____

STEP 1   Look for numbers that are one number apart.

STEP 2   Find the smaller number. Look for the doubles fact. Think about the sum.

Think
5 + 5 = 10

STEP 3   Add 1 to the doubles fact. Write the sum.

Think
10 + 1 = 11

5 + 6 = 11

(ON YOUR OWN)

Add using doubles plus one.

8 + 7 = _____

Think

Think

Practice

Building Skills

Add using doubles plus one.

1. 2 + 3 = _____

2. 7 + 6 = _____

3. 4 + 5 = _____

4. 9 + 8 = _____

Problem Solving

Solve.

5. Ali has 3 bears.
   Kendra has one more bear than Ali does.
   How many bears do the girls have in all?

_____

LESSON 30 · Adding from the Greater Number

One way to find sums is to add from the greater number.

Example

Add. 4 + 9 = _____

STEP 1 Find the greater number. Put a dot over the same number on the number line.

```
◄—+—+—+—+—+—+—+—+—+—●—+—+—+—+—+—+—+—+—+—+—►
   0  1  2  3  4  5  6  7  8  9 10 11 12 13 14 15 16 17 18 19 20
```

STEP 2 Look at the smaller number. Move that many places right.

```
◄—+—+—+—+—+—+—+—+—+—●⌒⌒⌒⌒+—+—+—+—+—+—+—+—►
   0  1  2  3  4  5  6  7  8  9 10 11 12 13 14 15 16 17 18 19 20
```

STEP 3 Find the end number. Circle the number. Write the sum.

```
◄—+—+—+—+—+—+—+—+—+—●⌒⌒⌒⌒⑬+—+—+—+—+—+—+—►
   0  1  2  3  4  5  6  7  8  9 10 11 12 13 14 15 16 17 18 19 20
```

4 + 9 = 13

(**ON YOUR OWN**)

Add from the greater number.

8 + 3 = _____

```
◄—+—+—+—+—+—+—+—+—+—+—+—+—+—+—+—+—+—+—+—+—►
   0  1  2  3  4  5  6  7  8  9 10 11 12 13 14 15 16 17 18 19 20
```

Name _____ Date _____

Practice

Building Skills

Add from the greater number.

1. $7 + 4 =$ _____

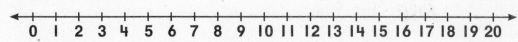

2. $6 + 9 =$ _____

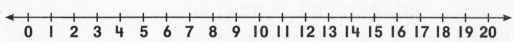

3. $8 + 5 =$ _____

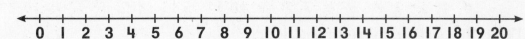

4. $9 + 3 =$ _____

0 1 2 3 4 5 6 7 8 9 10 11 12 13 14 15 16 17 18 19 20

More Practice Use the number lines on page 116 to write more addition sentences.

Problem Solving

Solve.

5. There are 7 jeans on the shelf.
The store clerk puts 6 more jeans on the shelf.
How many jeans are there in all?

_____

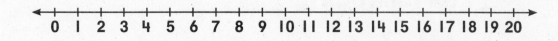

Name _____ Date _____

LESSON ③① Adding More Than Two Numbers

You can add more than two numbers. You can add down, or you can add up. You can also look for numbers whose sum equals 10.

Example

Add.   4
        2
      + 7

STEP 1   Look for two numbers whose
             sum equals 10.
               4
               2
             + 7

Think
No numbers have
a sum of 10.

STEP 2   Add down or add up.
               4
               2 ⟩9
             + 7

Think
7 + 2 = 9

STEP 3   Write the sum.
               4
               2 ⟩9
             + 7

Think
9 + 4 = 13

   4
   2
 + 7
  13

(**ON YOUR OWN**)

Add.   6
        4
      + 5

Unit 2: Lesson 31
Strengthening Math Skills: Addition and Subtraction, SV 9781419033971

Name _____ Date _____

Practice

Building Skills

Add.

1. 5
    1
    +4

2. 3
    7
    +2

3. 9
    5
    +1

4. 4
    3
    +6

5. 2
    2
    +7

6. 8
    2
    +3

7. 2
    4
    +8

8. 8
    6
    +1

9. 5
    4
    +9

Problem Solving

Solve.

10. Holly made a picture with pieces of different shapes.
    She used 8 triangles, 2 circles, and 2 rectangles.
    How many pieces did Holly use in all?

Name _____ Date _____

LESSON 32 Skip Counting

Sometimes you may have to add the same number many times.
You can skip count to add.

Count the fingers on the gloves.

___ ___ ___ ___ ___ ___

STEP 1 Add the numbers. Look for a pattern.

Think
The numbers end in 5 and 0.

 5   10   15   20   ___   ___

STEP 2 Finish skip counting using the pattern.

 5   10   15   20   25   30

(**ON YOUR OWN**)

Skip count.

 2   4   ___   ___   ___

___   ___   ___   ___   ___

70 Strengthening Math Skills: Addition and Subtraction, SV 9781419033971

Name _____ Date _____

Practice

Building Skills

Skip count.

1.

<u> 10 </u>   <u> 20 </u>   _____   _____   _____

_____   _____   _____   _____   _____

2.

<u> 3 </u>   <u> 6 </u>   _____   _____   _____

_____   _____   _____   _____   _____

Problem Solving

Solve.

3. Kai collects stamps.
He puts 6 stamps on each page.
He has 8 pages of stamps.
How many stamps does Kai have?
Show the skip count pattern.

_____ _____ _____ _____

_____ _____ _____ _____

Name _____ Date _____

LESSON ③③ Adding Facts to 18

Addition problems that have a sum of 18 or less are called **facts**.
You should know these facts very well.

Example

Here are some facts with 8. Add. Write the sums as quickly as you can.

5	8	9	0	8	8	7	8
+8	+2	+8	+8	+8	+4	+8	+6

STEP 1 Set a timer for 15 seconds.

STEP 2 Write the sums above as quickly as you can.

STEP 3 Stop when the timer goes off.

STEP 4 Check your work.

ON YOUR OWN

Add. Write the sums as quickly as you can.

3	5	9	8	7	6	4	9
+4	+7	+6	+5	+3	+6	+9	+9

Name _____ Date _____

Practice

Building Skills

Add. Write the sums as quickly as you can.

1.　　8　　　6　　　9　　　0　　　3　　　7　　　9
　　 + 3　　+ 8　　+ 4　　+ 4　　+ 3　　+ 6　　+ 5

2.　　7　　　5　　　2　　　9　　　2　　　6　　　5
　　 + 9　　+ 3　　+ 2　　+ 3　　+ 8　　+ 4　　+ 8

3.　　4　　　9　　　8　　　7　　　8　　　4　　　1
　　 + 8　　+ 1　　+ 8　　+ 5　　+ 9　　+ 2　　+ 8

4.　　9　　　3　　　1　　　8　　　0　　　5　　　5
　　 + 9　　+ 0　　+ 3　　+ 2　　+ 9　　+ 5　　+ 4

Problem Solving

Solve.

5.　There are 9 children swimming.
　　Soon 6 more children come to swim.
　　How many children are swimming now?

_____

Name _____ Date _____

Some addition facts and subtraction facts go together.

Example

Add. Then subtract.

$7 + 5 =$ _____

$12 - 5 =$ _____

STEP 1 Look at the addition sentence. Draw circles to show the first number. Draw more circles to show the other number.

STEP 2 How many circles in all? Write the sum.

$7 + 5 =$ __12__

STEP 3 Look at the subtraction sentence. Draw circles to show the first number. Draw an X on circles to show how many to take away.

○○○○○○○⊗⊗⊗⊗⊗

STEP 4 How many circles are left? Write the difference.

$12 - 5 =$ __7__

$7 + 5 = 12$ goes with $12 - 5 = 7$.

ON YOUR OWN

Add. Then subtract. Draw circles if you need to.

$8 + 6 =$ _____ $14 - 6 =$ _____

Strengthening Math Skills: Addition and Subtraction, SV 9781419033971

Unit 2: Lesson 34

Name _____ Date _____

Practice

Building Skills

Add. Then subtract. Draw circles if you need to.

1. 9 + 3 = _____   12 − 3 = _____

2. 8 + 7 = _____   15 − 7 = _____

3. 6 + 6 = _____   12 − 6 = _____

Problem Solving

Solve. Then show another fact that goes with the number sentence.

4. A baker makes 16 cakes.
She sells 8 of the cakes.
How many cakes are left?

_____   _____

Name _____ Date _____

LESSON 35 Subtracting Using Doubles Facts

Doubles facts can help you subtract.

Subtract. 16 − 8 = _____

STEP 1 Look at the first number. Decide if it is an even number. Remember that the sum of a doubles fact is always even.

Think
16 is an even number.

STEP 2 Look at the other number. Decide if the number is a doubles fact. Think of the sum of the doubles fact.

Think
8 + 8 = 16

STEP 3 Look at the subtraction sentence again. Decide if the doubles fact and the subtraction sentence go together. Write the difference.

16 − 8 = 8

Think
8 + 8 = 16
goes with
16 − 8 = 8

(**ON YOUR OWN**)

Subtract. Use a doubles fact.

10 − 5 = _____

_____

Strengthening Math Skills: Addition and Subtraction, SV 9781419033971

Unit 2: Lesson 35

Name _____ Date _____

Practice

Building Skills

Subtract. Use a doubles fact if you can.

1. $4 - 2 =$ _____

_____

2. $12 - 6 =$ _____

_____

3. $9 - 5 =$ _____

_____

4. $18 - 9 =$ _____

_____

5. $2 - 1 =$ _____

_____

6. $15 - 8 =$ _____

_____

7. $8 - 4 =$ _____

_____

8. $14 - 7 =$ _____

_____

Problem Solving

Solve. Write the doubles fact.

9. There are 6 seals on a rock.
Then 3 seals go for a swim.
How many seals are left on the rock?

_____

_____

Unit 2: Lesson 35
Strengthening Math Skills: Addition and Subtraction, SV 9781419033971

Name _____ Date _____

LESSON 36   Subtracting Using Addition Facts

Addition facts can help you subtract.

Example

Subtract. 17 − 8 = _____

STEP 1   Look at the two numbers. Write an addition sentence that goes with the subtraction sentence.

Think
___ + 8 = 17

STEP 2   Think of the number that completes the addition fact.

Think
9 + 8 = 17

STEP 3   Write the number as the difference. Check that the fact is true.

17 − 8 = ___9___

Think
Yes,
17 − 8 = 9.

17 − 8 = 9

(**ON YOUR OWN**)

Subtract. Use an addition fact to help you.

11 − 6 = _____

_____

Name _____ Date _____

Practice

Building Skills

Subtract. Use addition facts to help you.

1. $15 - 6 =$ _____

_____

2. $16 - 9 =$ _____

_____

3. $12 - 7 =$ _____

_____

4. $14 - 8 =$ _____

_____

5. $13 - 5 =$ _____

_____

6. $11 - 6 =$ _____

_____

7. $14 - 9 =$ _____

_____

8. $10 - 7 =$ _____

_____

Problem Solving

Solve. Write the addition fact that helped you.

9. Mr. Chang has 11 necklaces.
He sells 4 of the necklaces.
How many necklaces does Mr. Chang have left?

_____

_____

Name _____ Date _____

LESSON ③⑦ Mixed Operations to 18

Many times, there will be both addition and subtraction problems on a page. Look at the sign in each problem. The **+** sign means to add. The **−** sign means to subtract. Then find the sum or difference. Work the problems as quickly as you can.

Example

Add or subtract.

13	5	14	5
− 8	+ 2	− 6	+ 7

STEP 1 Look at the sign in the first problem. It means to subtract. Quickly write the difference.

STEP 2 Look at the sign in the next problem. It means to add. Quickly write the sum.

STEP 3 Repeat the steps. Look at each sign. Add or subtract. Quickly write the sums or differences.

13	5	14	5
− 8	+ 2	− 6	+ 7
5	7	8	12

(ON YOUR OWN)

Add or subtract.

9	17	5	13
+ 6	− 8	+ 0	− 7

Name _____ Date _____

Practice

Building Skills

Add or subtract.

| 1. | 13
− 6 | 8
+ 3 | 6
− 6 | 2
+ 9 | 7
+ 7 | 17
− 9 | 8
+ 6 |

| 2. | 11
− 7 | 14
− 8 | 8
+ 5 | 12
− 6 | 7
+ 6 | 15
− 9 | 5
+ 6 |

| 3. | 6
+ 4 | 17
− 8 | 10
− 8 | 13
− 8 | 4
+ 3 | 11
− 8 | 6
+ 6 |

| 4. | 9
+ 6 | 8
+ 4 | 6
− 0 | 9
+ 4 | 12
− 7 | 9
+ 9 | 11
− 5 |

Problem Solving

Solve.

5. There are 8 cows in the field and 7 in the barn.
How many cows are there altogether?

_____

Name _____ Date _____

LESSON **38** Missing Numbers

You can use fact families to help you find a missing number.

Example

Write the missing number. 8 + _____ = 15

STEP 1 Look at the two numbers in the sentence. Think of the addition and subtraction sentences for the fact family that includes those two numbers.

8 + _____ = 15   15 − 8 = _____

_____ + 8 = 15   15 − _____ = 8

STEP 2 Look for the number sentence where both numbers are to the left of the equals sign. Write the sum or difference.

15 − 8 = ___7___

STEP 3 The number you wrote will be the missing number. Write the number. Check the fact.

8 + 7 = 15

ON YOUR OWN

Write the missing number. Use fact families to help you.

13 − _____ = 5

_____ + _____ = _____   _____ − _____ = _____

_____ + _____ = _____   _____ − _____ = _____

Name _____ Date _____

Practice

Building Skills

Write the missing number. Use fact families to help you.

1. _____ + 3 = 9

_____ + _____ = _____   _____ − _____ = _____

_____ + _____ = _____   _____ − _____ = _____

2. 17 − _____ = 8

_____ + _____ = _____   _____ − _____ = _____

_____ + _____ = _____   _____ − _____ = _____

3. _____ − 8 = 6

_____ + _____ = _____   _____ − _____ = _____

_____ + _____ = _____   _____ − _____ = _____

4. 6 + _____ = 13

_____ + _____ = _____   _____ − _____ = _____

_____ + _____ = _____   _____ − _____ = _____

Problem Solving

Solve.

5. Farmer Brown has 11 horses.
There are 6 horses in the barn.
How many are out in the field?

_____

Name _____ Date _____

LESSON ③⑨ Building Numbers to 100

A cube equals 1 one. A rod equals 1 ten. You can use 10 ones to make 1 ten. Change 10 cubes for 1 rod.

Example

Write the number. 3 tens 17 ones = _____

STEP 1 How many ones? 17. Get 17 cubes. Put them in the ones column of the workmat.

HUNDREDS	TENS	ONES
		▫▫▫▫ ▫▫▫▫ ▫▫▫▫ ▫▫▫▫ ▫

3 tens   17 ones

STEP 2 How many tens? 3. Get 3 rods. Put them in the tens column of the workmat.

HUNDREDS	TENS	ONES
	‖‖‖	▫▫▫▫ ▫▫▫▫ ▫▫▫▫ ▫▫▫▫ ▫

3 tens   17 ones

STEP 3 Can you group 10 ones to make 1 ten? Change 10 cubes for a rod.

HUNDREDS	TENS	ONES
	‖‖‖	▣▣▣▣ ▣▣▣▣ ▣▣▫▫ ▫▫▫

3 tens   17 ones

Think
10 ones make 1 ten.

STEP 4 Put the rod in the tens column. Write the tens and ones. Write the number.

HUNDREDS	TENS	ONES
	‖‖‖‖	▫▫ ▫▫ ▫ ▫

3 tens   17 ones

__4__ tens __7__ ones

__47__

3 tens 17 ones is the same as 47.

Strengthening Math Skills: Addition and Subtraction, SV 9781419033971

Unit 3: Lesson 39

Name _____ Date _____

Practice

Building Skills

Write the number. Use the counters on page 114. Use the workmat on page 122.

1. 0 tens 17 ones

_____ tens _____ ones

_____

2. 1 ten 19 ones

_____ tens _____ ones

_____

3. 5 tens 15 ones

_____ tens _____ ones

_____

4. 7 tens 6 ones

_____ tens _____ ones

_____

5. 3 tens 10 ones

_____ tens _____ ones

_____

6. 8 tens 12 ones

_____ tens _____ ones

_____

7. 9 tens 4 ones

_____ tens _____ ones

_____

8. 6 tens 18 ones

_____ tens _____ ones

_____

Problem Solving

Solve.

9. There are 10 crayons in a box.
Carla buys 2 boxes of crayons.
She already has 13 crayons.
How many crayons does Carla have now?

_____ tens _____ ones

_____

Unit 3: Lesson 39

Strengthening Math Skills: Addition and Subtraction, SV 9781419033971

Name _____ Date _____

LESSON 40 Adding Tens

A place-value chart can help you add.

Add.

TENS	ONES
3	0
+ 1	0

STEP 1 Add the numbers in the ones column. Write the sum.

TENS	ONES
3	0
+ 1	0
	0

Think
0 + 0 = 0

STEP 2 Add the numbers in the tens column. Write the sum.

TENS	ONES
3	0
+ 1	0
4	0

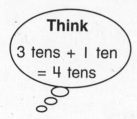

Think
3 tens + 1 ten
= 4 tens

ON YOUR OWN

Add.

TENS	ONES
2	0
+ 4	0

Strengthening Math Skills: Addition and Subtraction, SV 9781419033971

Unit 3: Lesson 40

Name _____ Date _____

Practice

Building Skills

Add.

1.

TENS	ONES
2	0
+2	0

2.

TENS	ONES
3	0
+1	0

3.

TENS	ONES
4	0
+3	0

4.

TENS	ONES
1	0
+7	0

5.

TENS	ONES
6	0
+2	0

6.

TENS	ONES
8	0
+1	0

7. 30
  + 30

8. 50
  + 20

9. 40
  + 0

More Practice Use the place-value charts on page 123 to write more problems.

Problem Solving

Solve.

10. There are 30 shirts on hangers.
    There are 20 shirts that are folded.
    How many shirts are there altogether?

TENS	ONES

Name _____ Date _____

LESSON 41 Adding 2-Digit Numbers

A place-value chart can help you add 2-digit numbers.

Example

Add.

TENS	ONES
2	6
+ I	3

STEP I Add the numbers in the ones column. Write the sum.

TENS	ONES
2	6
+ I	3
	9

Think
6 + 3 = 9

STEP 2 Add the numbers in the tens column. Write the sum.

TENS	ONES
2	6
+ I	3
3	9

Think
2 tens + I ten
= 3 tens

(**ON YOUR OWN**)

Add.

TENS	ONES
2	3
+ 2	4

Practice

Building Skills

Add.

1.

TENS	ONES
1	3
+	2

2.

TENS	ONES
3	5
+	4

3.

TENS	ONES
5	1
+	8

4.

TENS	ONES
3	2
+1	4

5.

TENS	ONES
1	2
+5	7

6.

TENS	ONES
4	4
+1	3

7. 50
     + 34

8. 41
     + 15

9. 36
     + 33

More Practice Use the place-value charts on page 123 to write more problems.

Problem Solving

Solve.

10. There are 25 baseballs in one box.
There are 43 baseballs in another box.
How many baseballs are there in all?

Name _____ Date _____

LESSON 42 Adding 2-Digit Numbers with Regrouping

Sometimes you need to regroup 10 ones to make 1 ten when you add.

Add.

TENS	ONES
4	3
+ 2	8

STEP 1 Add the ones. If there are 10 or more, regroup. Write the ones in the ones column. Write the tens in the box in the tens column.

TENS	ONES
☐	
4	3
+ 2	8
	1

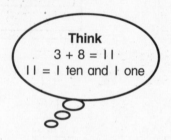

Think
3 + 8 = 11
11 = 1 ten and 1 one

STEP 2 Add the tens. Write the sum in the tens column.

TENS	ONES
1	
4	3
+ 2	8
7	1

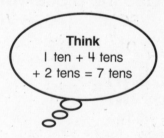

Think
1 ten + 4 tens
+ 2 tens = 7 tens

ON YOUR OWN

Add.

TENS	ONES
☐	
5	7
+ 2	6

Name _____ Date _____

Practice

Building Skills

Add.

1.
TENS	ONES
□	
3	9
+	4

2.
TENS	ONES
□	
2	6
+	9

3.
TENS	ONES
□	
8	3
+	7

4.
TENS	ONES
□	
2	2
+1	9

5.
TENS	ONES
□	
4	6
+4	6

6.
TENS	ONES
□	
7	9
+1	9

7. 57
     + 28

8. 17
     + 35

9. 41
     + 29

More Practice Use the place-value charts on page 123 to write more problems.

Problem Solving

Solve.

10. There are 42 windows on one building.
There are 28 windows on another building.
How many windows will the Clean Windows Company wash?

Strengthening Math Skills: Addition and Subtraction, SV 9781419033971

Name _____ Date _____

LESSON 43 Subtracting 2-Digit Numbers

A place-value chart can help you subtract 2-digit numbers.

Example

Subtract.

TENS	ONES
3	5
− 1	1

STEP 1 Subtract the numbers in the ones column. Write the difference.

TENS	ONES
3	5
− 1	1
	4

Think
5 − 1 = 4

STEP 2 Subtract the numbers in the tens column. Write the difference.

TENS	ONES
3	5
− 1	1
2	4

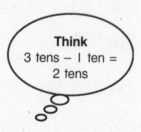

Think
3 tens − 1 ten =
2 tens

ON YOUR OWN

Subtract.

TENS	ONES
2	9
− 1	3

Strengthening Math Skills: Addition and Subtraction, SV 9781419033971

Unit 3: Lesson 43

Name _____ Date _____

Practice

Building Skills

Subtract.

1.
TENS	ONES
2	7
−	3

2.
TENS	ONES
4	8
−	6

3.
TENS	ONES
3	5
−	2

4.
TENS	ONES
4	5
−2	4

5.
TENS	ONES
8	7
−6	2

6.
TENS	ONES
3	9
−3	1

7.
$$48$$
$$-38$$

8.
$$69$$
$$-42$$

9.
$$75$$
$$-50$$

More Practice Use the place-value charts on page 123 to write more problems.

Problem Solving

Solve.

10. There are 25 butterfly cocoons in the garden. 15 of the cocoons change into butterflies. How many more cocoons will change to butterflies?

Name _____ Date _____

LESSON 44 Subtracting 2-Digit Numbers with Regrouping

Sometimes you need to regroup 1 ten to make 10 ones when you subtract.

Subtract.

STEP 1 Subtract the ones. If there are not enough ones, regroup. Cross out the number in the tens column. Write the new tens.

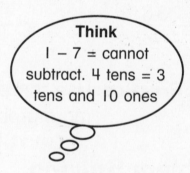

Think
1 − 7 = cannot subtract. 4 tens = 3 tens and 10 ones

STEP 2 Add the 10 ones to the ones. Cross out the number in the ones column. Write the new ones.

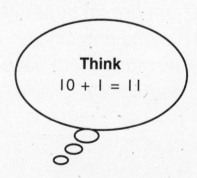

Think
10 + 1 = 11

Strengthening Math Skills: Addition and Subtraction, SV 9781419033971

Unit 3: Lesson 44

Example

STEP 3 Subtract the ones. Write the difference.

TENS	ONES
3	11
4̶	1̶
− 1	7
	4

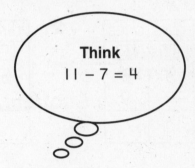

Think
11 − 7 = 4

STEP 4 Subtract the tens. Write the difference.

TENS	ONES
3	11
4̶	1̶
− 1	7
2	4

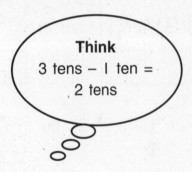

Think
3 tens − 1 ten = 2 tens

(**ON YOUR OWN**)

Subtract.

TENS	ONES
☐	☐
3	2
− 1	5

Name _____ Date _____

Practice

Building Skills

Subtract.

1.

TENS	ONES
☐	☐
3	8
–	9

2.

TENS	ONES
☐	☐
5	5
–	7

3.

TENS	ONES
☐	☐
2	2
–	4

4.

TENS	ONES
☐	☐
4	1
–1	3

5.

TENS	ONES
☐	☐
6	3
–1	8

6.

TENS	ONES
☐	☐
3	6
–2	7

7. 64
   −28

8. 75
   −48

9. 40
   −35

More Practice Use the place-value charts on page 123 to write more problems.

Problem Solving

Solve.

10. Amy takes 32 cupcakes to school.
   She gives away 24 cupcakes.
   How many cupcakes does Amy have left?

Unit 3: Lesson 44
Strengthening Math Skills: Addition and Subtraction, SV 9781419033971

Name _____ Date _____

LESSON (45) Checking Subtraction

You can add to make sure that the difference in a subtraction problem is correct.

Example

Subtract. Then check by adding.

$$\begin{array}{r} 4\ 4 \\ -\ 1\ 9 \end{array}\qquad +\ \underline{}$$

STEP 1 Subtract the ones.
Subtract the tens.
Regroup if you need to.

$$\begin{array}{r} {\scriptstyle 3\ \ 14} \\ \cancel{4}\ \cancel{4} \\ -\ 1\ 9 \\ \hline 2\ 5 \end{array}$$

STEP 2 Write the subtraction problem as an addition problem.

$$\begin{array}{r} {\scriptstyle 3\ \ 14} \\ \cancel{4}\ \cancel{4} \\ -\ 1\ 9 \\ \hline 2\ 5 \end{array}\qquad \begin{array}{r} 2\ 5 \\ +\ 1\ 9 \end{array}$$

STEP 3 Add. Regroup if you need to. The sum should be the first number in the subtraction problem.

$$\begin{array}{r} {\scriptstyle 3\ \ 14} \\ \cancel{4}\ \cancel{4} \\ -\ 1\ 9 \\ \hline 2\ 5 \end{array}\qquad \begin{array}{r} {\scriptstyle 1} \\ 2\ 5 \\ +\ 1\ 9 \\ \hline 4\ 4 \end{array}$$

The subtraction problem is correct. The addition problem shows it is correct.

(**ON YOUR OWN**)

Subtract. Then check by adding.

$$\begin{array}{r} 3\ 1 \\ -\ 1\ 3 \end{array}\qquad +\ \underline{}$$

Unit 3: Lesson 45
Strengthening Math Skills: Addition and Subtraction, SV 9781419033971

Name _____   Date _____

Practice

Building Skills

Subtract. Then check by adding.

1.   44 _____
     −8 + _____

2.   39 _____
     −7 + _____

3.   46 _____
     −5 + _____

4.   58 _____
     −13 + _____

5.   43 _____
     −26 + _____

6.   84 _____
     −49 + _____

7.   29 _____
     −17 + _____

8.   92 _____
     −23 + _____

9.   74 _____
     −57 + _____

10. 59 _____
     −28 + _____

11. 44 _____
     −20 + _____

12. 60 _____
     −38 + _____

Problem Solving

Solve.

13. There are 26 campsites in a park.
     18 sites have tents.
     How many sites do not have tents?

Name _____ Date _____

LESSON 46 Adding 3-Digit Numbers

A place-value chart can help you add 3-digit numbers.

Example

Add.

HUNDREDS	TENS	ONES
1	4	5
+	2	4

STEP 1 Add the numbers in the ones column. Write the sum.

HUNDREDS	TENS	ONES
1	4	5
+	2	4
		9

Think
$5 + 4 = 9$

STEP 2 Add the numbers in the tens column. Write the sum.

HUNDREDS	TENS	ONES
1	4	5
+	2	4
	6	9

Think
4 tens + 2 tens
= 6 tens

STEP 3 Add the numbers in the hundreds column. Write the sum.

HUNDREDS	TENS	ONES
1	4	5
+	2	4
1	6	9

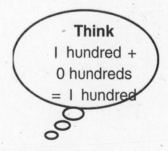

Think
1 hundred +
0 hundreds
= 1 hundred

Name _____ Date _____

Practice

Building Skills

Add.

1.

HUNDREDS	TENS	ONES
2	6	4
+	1	3

2.

HUNDREDS	TENS	ONES
1	5	6
+	3	0

3.

HUNDREDS	TENS	ONES
7	3	4
+	5	1

4.

HUNDREDS	TENS	ONES
1	1	7
+1	0	1

5.

HUNDREDS	TENS	ONES
4	4	4
+1	2	5

6.

HUNDREDS	TENS	ONES
3	1	2
+2	5	6

7.   524
        +313

8.   410
        +125

9.   872
        +127

Problem Solving

Solve.

10. The school ordered 425 boxes of milk.
It ordered 320 boxes of fruit juice.
How many boxes of drinks did the school order in all?

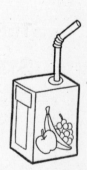

Strengthening Math Skills: Addition and Subtraction, SV 9781419033971

Adding 3-Digit Numbers with Regrouping

LESSON 47

Sometimes you need to regroup when you add. You might regroup 10 ones to make 1 ten. You might regroup 10 tens to make 1 hundred.

Example

Add.

HUNDREDS	TENS	ONES
3	6	8
+ 1	5	4

STEP 1 Add the ones. If there are 10 or more, regroup. Write the ones in the ones column. Write the tens in the box in the tens column.

HUNDREDS	TENS	ONES
	☐	
3	6	8
+ 1	5	4
		2

Think
8 + 4 = 12
12 = 1 ten and 2 ones

STEP 2 Add the tens. If there are 10 or more, regroup. Write the tens in the tens column. Write the hundreds in the box in the hundreds column.

HUNDREDS	TENS	ONES
☐	☐	
3	6	8
+ 1	5	4
2	2	

Think
1 fen + 6 tens
+ 5 tens = 12 tens
12 tens = 1 hundred
and 2 tens

Example

STEP 3 Add the hundreds. Write the hundreds in the hundreds column.

HUNDREDS	TENS	ONES
☐ 1		
3	6	8
+ 1	5	4
5	2	2

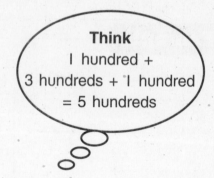

Think
1 hundred +
3 hundreds + 1 hundred
= 5 hundreds

ON YOUR OWN

Add.

HUNDREDS	TENS	ONES
☐	☐	
4	3	9
+ 2	7	6

Unit 3: Lesson 47
Strengthening Math Skills: Addition and Subtraction, SV 9781419033971

Name _____ Date _____

Practice

Building Skills

Add.

1.

HUNDREDS	TENS	ONES
☐	☐	
3	2	7
+	5	4

2.

HUNDREDS	TENS	ONES
☐	☐	
4	2	9
+	9	6

3.

HUNDREDS	TENS	ONES
☐	☐	
2	6	0
+	7	7

4.   413
     +319

5.   187
     +212

6.   637
     +266

More Practice Use the place-value charts on page 123 to write more problems.

Problem Solving

Solve.

7. Lamar School had a book drive for the library.
Mr. Garza's class collected 257 books,
and Mrs. Wai's class collected 306 books.
How many books did the classes collect in all?

Name _____ Date _____

LESSON **48** Subtracting 3-Digit Numbers

A place-value chart can help you subtract 3-digit numbers.

Example

Subtract.

HUNDREDS	TENS	ONES
2	6	8
– 1	4	7

STEP 1 Subtract the numbers in the ones column.
Write the difference.

HUNDREDS	TENS	ONES
2	6	8
– 1	4	7
		1

Think
8 – 7 = 1

STEP 2 Subtract the numbers in the tens column.
Write the difference.

HUNDREDS	TENS	ONES
2	6	8
– 1	4	7
	2	1

Think
6 tens – 4 tens
= 2 tens

STEP 3 Subtract the numbers in the hundreds column.
Write the difference.

HUNDREDS	TENS	ONES
2	6	8
– 1	4	7
1	2	1

Think
2 hundreds
– 1 hundred
= 1 hundred

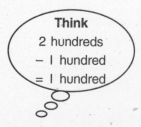

Strengthening Math Skills: Addition and Subtraction, SV 9781419033971

Unit 3: Lesson 48

Name _____ Date _____

Practice

Building Skills

Subtract.

1.

HUNDREDS	TENS	ONES
4	2	7
–	1	5

2.

HUNDREDS	TENS	ONES
3	9	8
–	3	6

3.

HUNDREDS	TENS	ONES
5	6	4
–	2	4

4.

HUNDREDS	TENS	ONES
3	5	4
–1	2	3

5.

HUNDREDS	TENS	ONES
6	3	6
–3	2	0

6.

HUNDREDS	TENS	ONES
2	7	8
–1	7	5

7.   795
       –124

8.   629
       –603

9.   521
       –411

Problem Solving

Solve.

10. Janelle is reading a book that has 158 pages.
She has read 46 pages.
How many pages does Janelle have left to read?

Unit 3: Lesson 48
Strengthening Math Skills: Addition and Subtraction, SV 9781419033971

LESSON 49

Subtracting 3-Digit Numbers with Regrouping

Sometimes you need to regroup when you subtract. You might regroup 1 hundred as 10 tens. You might regroup 1 ten to make 10 ones.

Example

Subtract.

HUNDREDS	TENS	ONES
☐	☐	☐
3	5	4
−1	6	7

STEP 1 Subtract the ones. If there are not enough ones, regroup. Cross out the number in the tens column. Write the new tens in the box in the tens column.

HUNDREDS	TENS	ONES
☐	4	☐
3	5̸	4
−1	6	7

Think
4 − 7 = cannot subtract. 5 tens = 4 tens and 10 ones

STEP 2 Add the 10 ones to the ones. Cross out the number in the ones column. Write the new ones in the box in the ones column.

HUNDREDS	TENS	ONES
☐	4	14
3	5̸	4̸
−1	6	7

Think
10 + 4 = 14

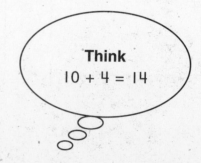

Strengthening Math Skills: Addition and Subtraction, SV 9781419033971

Unit 3: Lesson 49

Name _____ Date _____

Example

STEP 3 Subtract the ones. Write the difference.

HUNDREDS	TENS	ONES
□	4	14
3	5̶	4̶
− 1	6	7
		7

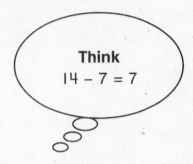

Think
14 − 7 = 7

STEP 4 Subtract the tens. If there are not enough tens, regroup. Cross out the numbers in the hundreds and tens columns. Write the new numbers. Subtract the tens. Write the difference.

HUNDREDS	TENS	ONES
2	14 / 4̶	14
3̶	5̶	4̶
− 1	6	7
	8	7

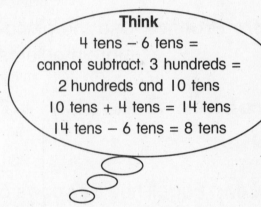

Think
4 tens − 6 tens =
cannot subtract. 3 hundreds =
2 hundreds and 10 tens
10 tens + 4 tens = 14 tens
14 tens − 6 tens = 8 tens

STEP 5 Subtract the hundreds. Write the difference.

HUNDREDS	TENS	ONES
2	14 / 4̶	14
3̶	5̶	4̶
− 1	6	7
1	8	7

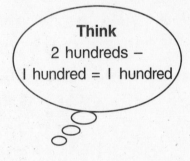

Think
2 hundreds −
1 hundred = 1 hundred

Unit 3: Lesson 49
Strengthening Math Skills: Addition and Subtraction, SV 9781419033971

Name _____ Date _____

Practice

Building Skills

Subtract.

1.

HUNDREDS	TENS	ONES
☐	☐	☐
2	6	8
−	7	6

2.

HUNDREDS	TENS	ONES
☐	☐	☐
7	4	7
−	3	9

3.

HUNDREDS	TENS	ONES
☐	☐	☐
4	1	3
−	4	8

4. 324
  −145

5. 561
  −189

6. 722
  −376

More Practice Use the place-value charts on page 123 to write more problems.

Problem Solving

Solve.

7. Mr. Farrell had 327 cows at the Rocking R Ranch. He moved 168 cows to the Sleepy L Ranch. How many cows were left at the Rocking R Ranch?

Name _____ Date _____

LESSON 50 Subtracting Across Zero

Some subtraction problems have zeros in the tens and ones places.
You will need to regroup to subtract.

Example

Subtract.

HUNDREDS	TENS	ONES
☐	☐	☐
4	0	0
− 1	3	9

STEP 1 Subtract the ones. If there are not enough ones, regroup. If there are no tens either, regroup 1 hundred to make 10 tens. Cross out the numbers in the hundreds and tens columns. Write the new hundreds and tens.

HUNDREDS	TENS	ONES
3	10	
4̶	0̶	0
− 1	3	9

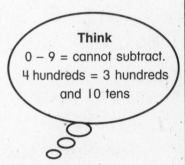

Think
0 − 9 = cannot subtract.
4 hundreds = 3 hundreds and 10 tens

STEP 2 Regroup 1 ten to make 10 ones. Cross out the number in the tens column. Write the new tens and ones.

HUNDREDS	TENS	ONES
	9	
3	1̶0̶	10
4̶	0̶	0̶
− 1	3	9

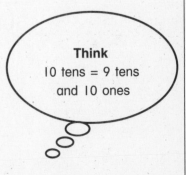

Think
10 tens = 9 tens and 10 ones

Example

STEP 3 Subtract the ones. Write the difference.

HUNDREDS	TENS	ONES
[3] ~~4~~ − 1	9 [~~10~~] ~~0~~ 3	[10] ~~0~~ 9
		1

STEP 4 Subtract the tens. Write the difference.

HUNDREDS	TENS	ONES
[3] ~~4~~ − 1	9 [~~10~~] ~~0~~ 3	[10] ~~0~~ 9
	6	1

STEP 5 Subtract the hundreds. Write the difference.

HUNDREDS	TENS	ONES
[3] ~~4~~ − 1	9 [~~10~~] ~~0~~ 3	[10] ~~0~~ 9
2	6	1

ON YOUR OWN

Subtract.

HUNDREDS	TENS	ONES
☐	☐	☐
7 − 3	0 5	0 1

Name _____   Date _____

Practice

Building Skills

Subtract.

1.	HUNDREDS	TENS	ONES
	☐	☐	☐
	2	0	0
−		4	3

2.	HUNDREDS	TENS	ONES
	☐	☐	☐
	5	0	0
−		7	2

3.	HUNDREDS	TENS	ONES
	☐	☐	☐
	4	0	0
−2		5	8

4. $\begin{array}{r} 600 \\ -306 \\ \hline \end{array}$

5. $\begin{array}{r} 300 \\ -211 \\ \hline \end{array}$

6. $\begin{array}{r} 900 \\ -594 \\ \hline \end{array}$

More Practice Use the place-value charts on page 123 to write more problems.

Problem Solving

Solve.

7. There are 300 pencils in a box.
   The school store sells 125 of them in one week.
   How many pencils are left?

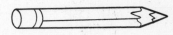

Unit 3: Lesson 50
Strengthening Math Skills: Addition and Subtraction, SV 9781419033971

Name _____ Date _____

LESSON 51 Mixed Operations

Many times, there will be addition and subtraction problems on a page. Look at the sign in each problem. The **+** sign means to add. The **–** sign means to subtract. Then find the sum or difference.

Example

Add or subtract.

$$
\begin{array}{r} 156 \\ +\ 14 \\ \hline \end{array}
\qquad
\begin{array}{r} 608 \\ -\ 27 \\ \hline \end{array}
\qquad
\begin{array}{r} 436 \\ -315 \\ \hline \end{array}
\qquad
\begin{array}{r} 672 \\ +285 \\ \hline \end{array}
$$

STEP 1   Look at the sign in the first problem. It means to add. Write the sum.

STEP 2   Look at the sign in the next problem. It means to subtract. Write the difference.

STEP 3   Repeat the steps. Look at each sign. Add or subtract. Write the sums or differences.

$$
\begin{array}{r} {}^{1} \\ 156 \\ +\ 14 \\ \hline 170 \end{array}
\qquad
\begin{array}{r} {}^{5\,10} \\ \cancel{608} \\ -\ 27 \\ \hline 581 \end{array}
\qquad
\begin{array}{r} 436 \\ -315 \\ \hline 121 \end{array}
\qquad
\begin{array}{r} {}^{1} \\ 672 \\ +285 \\ \hline 957 \end{array}
$$

(ON YOUR OWN)

Add or subtract.

$$
\begin{array}{r} 200 \\ -\ 35 \\ \hline \end{array}
\qquad
\begin{array}{r} 679 \\ +\ 94 \\ \hline \end{array}
\qquad
\begin{array}{r} 546 \\ -356 \\ \hline \end{array}
\qquad
\begin{array}{r} 363 \\ +600 \\ \hline \end{array}
$$

Strengthening Math Skills: Addition and Subtraction, SV 9781419033971

Unit 3: Lesson 51

Name _____ Date _____

Practice

Building Skills

Add or subtract.

1.
```
  62
+ 23
```

2.
```
  75
- 28
```

3.
```
  34
- 18
```

4.
```
  86
+ 74
```

5.
```
  716
-  71
```

6.
```
  654
+  87
```

7.
```
  469
+ 372
```

8.
```
  300
- 108
```

9.
```
  243
+ 381
```

10.
```
  723
- 246
```

11.
```
  126
+ 347
```

12.
```
  972
- 285
```

13.
```
  835
- 386
```

14.
```
  538
- 369
```

15.
```
  452
- 174
```

16.
```
  600
- 576
```

Problem Solving

Solve.

17. A kite company sold 245 kites in February.
It sold 629 kites in March.
How many kites did it sell altogether?

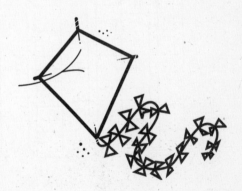

Unit 3: Lesson 51
Strengthening Math Skills: Addition and Subtraction, SV 9781419033971

Counters

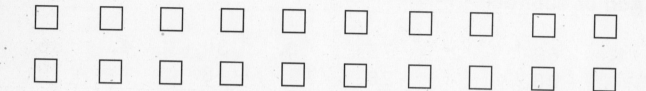

Cubes

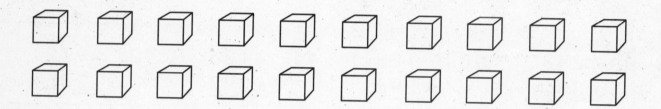

Rods

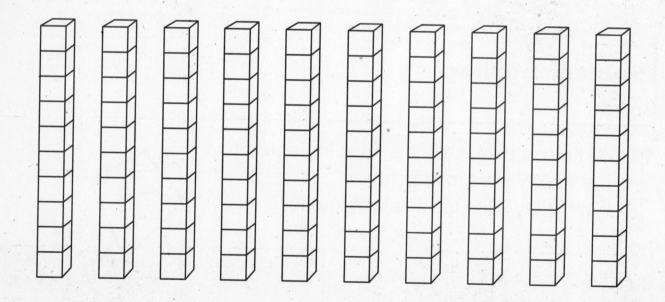

Name _____ Date _____

Addition Workmats

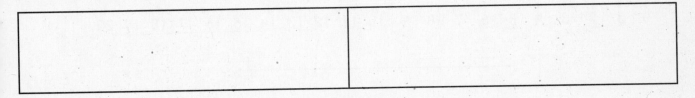

_____ + _____ = _____

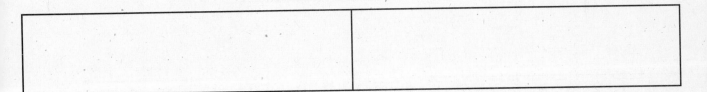

_____ + _____ = _____

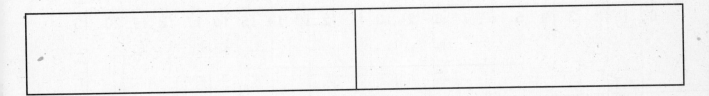

_____ + _____ = _____

_____ + _____ = _____

Graphic Organizers
Strengthening Math Skills: Addition and Subtraction, SV 9781419033971

Number Lines

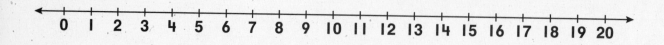

0 1 2 3 4 5 6 7 8 9 10 11 12 13 14 15 16 17 18 19 20

_____

0 1 2 3 4 5 6 7 8 9 10 11 12 13 14 15 16 17 18 19 20

_____

0 1 2 3 4 5 6 7 8 9 10 11 12 13 14 15 16 17 18 19 20

_____

0 1 2 3 4 5 6 7 8 9 10 11 12 13 14 15 16 17 18 19 20

_____

0 1 2 3 4 5 6 7 8 9 10 11 12 13 14 15 16 17 18 19 20

_____

0 1 2 3 4 5 6 7 8 9 10 11 12 13 14 15 16 17 18 19 20

_____

Strengthening Math Skills: Addition and Subtraction, SV 9781419033971

Graphic Organizers

Numbered Circles

⑩	⑩	⑩	⑩	⑩	⑩
⑨	⑨	⑨	⑨	⑨	⑨
⑧	⑧	⑧	⑧	⑧	⑧
⑦	⑦	⑦	⑦	⑦	⑦
⑥	⑥	⑥	⑥	⑥	⑥
⑤	⑤	⑤	⑤	⑤	⑤
④	④	④	④	④	④
③	③	③	③	③	③
②	②	②	②	②	②
①	①	①	①	①	①

Graphic Organizers
Strengthening Math Skills: Addition and Subtraction, SV 9781419033971

Name _____ Date _____

Addition Table

+	0	1	2	3	4	5	6	7	8	9
0	0	1	2	3	4	5	6	7	8	9
1	1	2	3	4	5	6	7	8	9	10
2	2	3	4	5	6	7	8	9	10	11
3	3	4	5	6	7	8	9	10	11	12
4	4	5	6	7	8	9	10	11	12	13
5	5	6	7	8	9	10	11	12	13	14
6	6	7	8	9	10	11	12	13	14	15
7	7	8	9	10	11	12	13	14	15	16
8	8	9	10	11	12	13	14	15	16	17
9	9	10	11	12	13	14	15	16	17	18

Strengthening Math Skills: Addition and Subtraction, SV 9781419033971

Graphic Organizers

Subtraction Workmats

_____ - _____ = _____

_____ - _____ = _____

_____ - _____ = _____

_____ - _____ = _____

Name _____ Date _____

Ten Frames

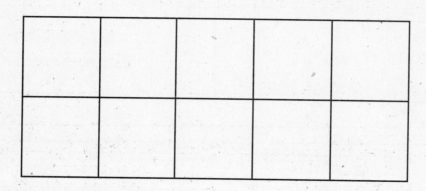

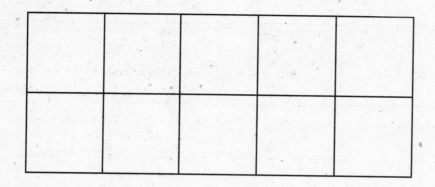

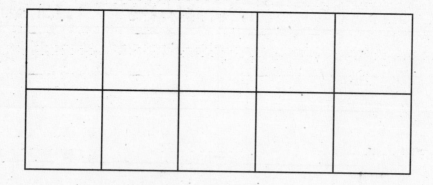

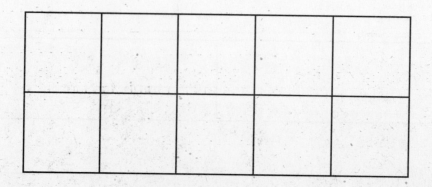

Strengthening Math Skills: Addition and Subtraction, SV 9781419033971

Graphic Organizers

Name _____ Date _____

Solving Addition and Subtraction Word Problems

What I Know

Part of a Group Number _____

Part of a Group Number _____

Total Number _____

Clue Words _____

I will add.   I will subtract.

What I Think the Number Sentence Will Be

   ◯      =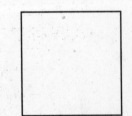

Number or Total   **Sign**   **Number**   **Total or Number**

My Work

Solve _____

Graphic Organizers
Strengthening Math Skills: Addition and Subtraction, SV 9781419033971

Name _____ Date _____

Place-Value Workmat

Ones	
Tens	
Hundreds	

Place-Value Charts

HUNDREDS	TENS	ONES
☐	☐	☐
○		

HUNDREDS	TENS	ONES
☐	☐	☐
○		

HUNDREDS	TENS	ONES
☐	☐	☐
○		

HUNDREDS	TENS	ONES
☐	☐	☐
○		

HUNDREDS	TENS	ONES
☐	☐	☐
○		

HUNDREDS	TENS	ONES
☐	☐	☐
○		

HUNDREDS	TENS	ONES
☐	☐	☐
○		

HUNDREDS	TENS	ONES
☐	☐	☐
○		

Graphic Organizers
Strengthening Math Skills: Addition and Subtraction, SV 9781419033971

ASSESSMENT

PAGE 5
1. 9
2. 8
3. 7
4. 8
5. 12
6. 18
7. 19
8. 38
9. 12
10. 91
11. 313
12. 585
13. 620
14. 192
15. $4 + 5 = 9, 5 + 4 = 9, 9 - 5 = 4, 9 - 4 = 5$

PAGE 6
1. $6 - 4 = 2$
2. $9 + 3 = 12$
3. $36 - 18 = 18$
4. $47 + 39 = 86$
5. $329 + 221 = 550$

LESSON 1

PAGE 9
1. 2 in, 1 joins, 3 in all
2. 5 in, 1 joins, 6 in all
3. 2 in, 2 join, 4 in all
4. 6 in all

LESSON 2

ON YOUR OWN (PAGE 10): $1 + 4 = 5$
PAGE 11
1. $1 + 1 = 2$
2. $3 + 2 = 5$
3. $2 + 2 = 4$
4. $3 + 3 = 6$

LESSON 3

ON YOUR OWN (PAGE 12): $2 + 4 = 6$
PAGE 13
1. 4
2. 6
3. 5
4. 6
5. $2 + 2 = 4$

LESSON 4

ON YOUR OWN (PAGE 14): $4 + 4 = 8$
PAGE 15
1. 9
2. 7
3. 8
4. 9
5. $4 + 2 = 6$

LESSON 5

ON YOUR OWN (PAGE 16): $7 + 3 = 10$
PAGE 17
1. 5
2. 10
3. 9
4. 8
5. $4 + 4 = 8$

LESSON 6

ON YOUR OWN (PAGE 19): $6 + 1 = 7, 1 + 6 = 7$
PAGE 19
1. $3 + 5 = 8, 5 + 3 = 8$
2. $9 + 1 = 10, 1 + 9 = 10$
3. $4 + 3 = 7, 3 + 4 = 7$
4. $2 + 6 = 8, 6 + 2 = 8$
5. $7 + 2 = 9, 2 + 7 = 9$

LESSON 7

ON YOUR OWN (PAGE 20): $0 + 6 = 6$
PAGE 21
1. 7
2. 1
3. 3
4. 9
5. $2 + 0 = 2$

LESSON 8

ON YOUR OWN (PAGE 23): Children write $5 + 3 = 8$ across and down.
PAGE 23

Children write each number sentence across and down.
1. $4 + 4 = 8$
2. $6 + 3 = 9$
3. $3 + 4 = 7$

LESSON 9

ON YOUR OWN (PAGE 24): $8 + 1 = 9$
PAGE 25
1. 7
2. 7
3. 10
4. 8
5. $6 + 3 = 9$

LESSON 10

ON YOUR OWN (PAGE 26): $2 + 4 = 6$
PAGE 27

1. 7   2. 10   3. 10
4. 8   5. $5 + 2 = 7$

LESSON 11

ON YOUR OWN (PAGE 28): 7, 9, 6, 5, 10, 10, 6
PAGE 29

1. 7, 7, 8, 6, 9, 10, 9   2. 8, 10, 10, 0, 5, 6, 6
3. 9, 6, 8, 7, 10, 10, 9   4. 4, 3, 4, 8, 8, 10, 10
5. $3 + 6 = 9$

LESSON 12

ON YOUR OWN (PAGE 30): 5, 3, 2
PAGE 31

1. 3 in all, 1 goes away, 2 are left
2. 4 in all, 1 goes away, 3 are left
3. 6 in all, 1 goes away, 5 are left
4. 4 in all, 1 goes away, 3 are left

LESSON 13

ON YOUR OWN (PAGE 32): $4 - 2 = 2$
PAGE 33

1. $5 - 4 = 1$ 2. $4 - 3 = 1$
3. $3 - 2 = 1$ 4. $5 - 3 = 2$

LESSON 14

ON YOUR OWN (PAGE 34): $5 - 4 = 1$
PAGE 35

1. 1   2. 2   3. 2
4. 1   5. $5 - 1 = 4$

LESSON 15

ON YOUR OWN (PAGE 36): $6 - 2 = 4$
PAGE 37

1. 2   2. 7   3. 2
4. 5   5. $7 - 3 = 4$

LESSON 16

ON YOUR OWN (PAGE 38): $7 - 2 = 5$
PAGE 39

1. 3   2. 2   3. 1
4. 5   5. $6 - 4 = 2$

LESSON 17

ON YOUR OWN (PAGE 40): $4 - 4 = 0$
PAGE 41

1. 0   2. 0   3. 0
4. 0   5. $5 - 5 = 0$

LESSON 18

ON YOUR OWN (PAGE 42): $2 - 0 = 2$
PAGE 43

1. 1   2. 6   3. 4
4. 8   5. $9 - 0 = 9$

LESSON 19

ON YOUR OWN (PAGE 45): $7 - 3 = 4$
PAGE 45

Children write each number sentence across and down.
1. $8 - 2 = 6$ 2. $6 - 4 = 2$ 3. $8 - 6 = 2$

LESSON 20

ON YOUR OWN (PAGE 46): $7 - 3 = 4$
PAGE 47

1. 2   2. 5   3. 4
4. 7   5. $9 - 2 = 7$

LESSON 21

ON YOUR OWN (PAGE 48): $8 - 3 = 5$
PAGE 49

1. 3   2. 6
3. 6   4. $8 - 2 = 6$

LESSON 22

ON YOUR OWN (PAGE 50): 8 − 4 = 4
PAGE 51

1. 3	**2.** 1	**3.** 4
4. 2	**5.** 5 − 3 = 2	

LESSON 23

ON YOUR OWN (PAGE 52): 3, 5, 3, 4, 0, 2, 3
PAGE 53

1. 3, 2, 2, 2, 1, 3, 1	**2.** 2, 3, 1, 1, 2, 0, 4
3. 2, 5, 2, 8, 5, 1, 3	**4.** 8, 5, 1, 3, 5, 3, 4
5. 10 − 7 = 3	

LESSON 24

ON YOUR OWN (PAGE 54): 10, 6, 4, 9
PAGE 55

1. 9, 2, 4, 10, 10, 7, 4	**2.** 2, 8, 3, 10, 0, 8, 2
3. 10, 8, 4, 6, 4, 1, 7	**4.** 3, 6, 8, 9, 7, 4, 1
5. 8 − 4 = 4	

LESSON 25

ON YOUR OWN (PAGE 56): 6 + 2 = 8, 2 + 6 = 8,
8 − 6 = 2, 8 − 2 = 6

PAGE 57

1. 4 + 1 = 5, 1 + 4 = 5, 5 − 1 = 4, 5 − 4 = 1
2. 8 + 2 = 10, 2 + 8 = 10, 10 − 8 = 2, 10 − 2 = 8
3. 3 + 4 = 7, 4 + 3 = 7, 7 − 4 = 3, 7 − 3 = 4
4. 6 + 3 = 9, 3 + 6 = 9, 9 − 6 = 3, 9 − 3 = 6
5. 7 + 1 = 8, 1 + 7 = 8, 8 − 1 = 7, 8 − 7 = 1

LESSON 26

ON YOUR OWN (PAGE 58): 1 ten, 7 ones, 17 in all
PAGE 59

1. 1 ten, 1 one, 11 in all
2. 1 ten, 5 ones, 15 in all
3. 1 ten, 8 ones, 18 in all
4. 1 ten, 3 ones, 13 in all
5. 1 ten, 6 ones, 16 in all

LESSON 27

ON YOUR OWN (PAGE 60): 9 + 7 = 16
PAGE 61

1. 15	**2.** 12
3. 14	**4.** 8 + 5 = 13

LESSON 28

ON YOUR OWN (PAGE 62): 9 + 9 = 18
PAGE 63

1. 6	**2.** 14
3. 10	**4.** 4 + 4 = 8

LESSON 29

ON YOUR OWN (PAGE 64): 8 + 7 = 15
PAGE 65

1. 5	**2.** 13	**3.** 9
4. 17	**5.** 3 + 4 = 7	

LESSON 30

ON YOUR OWN (PAGE 66): 8 + 3 = 11
PAGE 67

1. 11	**2.** 15	**3.** 13
4. 12	**5.** 7 + 6 = 13	

LESSON 31

ON YOUR OWN (PAGE 68): 6 + 4 + 5 = 15
PAGE 69

1. 10	**2.** 12	**3.** 15	**4.** 13
5. 11	**6.** 13	**7.** 14	**8.** 15
9. 18	**10.** 8 + 2 + 2 = 12		

LESSON 32

ON YOUR OWN (PAGE 70): 2, 4, 6, 8, 10, 12, 14, 16, 18, 20
PAGE 71

1. 10, 20, 30, 40, 50, 60, 70, 80, 90, 100
2. 3, 6, 9, 12, 15, 18, 21, 24, 27, 30
3. 6, 12, 18, 24, 30, 36, 42, 48

LESSON 33

ON YOUR OWN (PAGE 72): 7, 12, 15, 13, 10, 12, 13, 18
PAGE 73

1. 11, 14, 13, 4, 6, 13, 14
2. 16, 8, 4, 12, 10, 10, 13
3. 12, 10, 16, 12, 17, 6, 9
4. 18, 3, 4, 10, 9, 10, 9
5. 9 + 6 = 15

LESSON 34

ON YOUR OWN (PAGE 74): 8 + 6 = 14, 14 − 6 = 8
PAGE 75

1. 12, 9
2. 15, 8
3. 12, 6
4. 16 − 8 = 8, 8 + 8 = 16

LESSON 35

ON YOUR OWN (PAGE 76): 10 − 5 = 5, 5 + 5 = 10
PAGE 77

1. 4 − 2 = 2, 2 + 2 = 4
2. 12 − 6 = 6, 6 + 6 = 12
3. 9 − 5 = 4
4. 18 − 9 = 9, 9 + 9 = 18
5. 2 − 1 = 1, 1 + 1 = 2
6. 15 − 8 = 7
7. 8 − 4 = 4, 4 + 4 = 8
8. 14 − 7 = 7, 7 + 7 = 14
9. 6 − 3 = 3, 3 + 3 = 6

LESSON 36

ON YOUR OWN (PAGE 78): 11 − 6 = 5, 5 + 6 = 11
PAGE 79

1. 15 − 6 = 9, 9 + 6 = 15
2. 16 − 9 = 7, 7 + 9 = 16
3. 12 − 7 = 5, 5 + 7 = 12
4. 14 − 8 = 6, 6 + 8 = 14
5. 13 − 5 = 8, 8 + 5 = 13
6. 11 − 6 = 5, 5 + 6 = 11
7. 14 − 9 = 5, 5 + 9 = 14
8. 10 − 7 = 3, 3 + 7 = 10
9. 11 − 4 = 7, 7 + 4 = 11

LESSON 37

ON YOUR OWN (PAGE 80): 15, 9, 5, 6
PAGE 81

1. 7, 11, 0, 11, 14, 8, 14
2. 4, 6, 13, 6, 13, 6, 11
3. 10, 9, 2, 5, 7, 3, 12
4. 15, 12, 6, 13, 5, 18, 6
5. 8 + 7 = 15

LESSON 38

ON YOUR OWN (PAGE 82):

5 + _____ = 13, _____ + 5 = 13, 13 − 5 = 8,
13 − _____ = 5; Answer: 13 − 8 = 5

PAGE 83

1. _____ + 3 = 9, 3 + _____ = 9, 9 − 3 = 6, 9 − _____ = 3;
Answer: 6 + 3 = 9
2. 8 + _____ = 17, _____ + 8 = 17, 17 − 8 = 9, 17 − _____ = 8;
Answer: 17 − 9 = 8
3. 8 + 6 = 14, 6 + 8 = 14, _____ − 8 = 6, _____ − 6 = 8;
Answer: 14 − 8 = 6
4. 6 + _____ = 13, _____ + 6 = 13, 13 − 6 = 7, 13 − _____ = 6;
Answer: 6 + 7 = 13
5. 11 − 6 = 5

LESSON 39

PAGE 85

1. 1 ten 7 ones, 17
2. 2 tens 9 ones, 29
3. 6 tens 5 ones, 65
4. 7 tens 6 ones, 76
5. 4 tens 0 ones, 40
6. 9 tens 2 ones, 92
7. 9 tens 4 ones, 94
8. 7 tens 8 ones, 78
9. 2 tens 13 ones, 33

LESSON 40

ON YOUR OWN (PAGE 86): 20 + 40 = 60
PAGE 87

1. 40
2. 40
3. 70
4. 80
5. 80
6. 90
7. 60
8. 70
9. 40
10. 30 + 20 = 50

LESSON 41

ON YOUR OWN (PAGE 88): 23 + 24 = 47
PAGE 89

1. 15
2. 39
3. 59
4. 46
5. 69
6. 57
7. 84
8. 56
9. 69
10. 25 + 43 = 68

LESSON 42

ON YOUR OWN (PAGE 90): 57 + 26 = 83
PAGE 91

1. 43	**2.** 35	**3.** 90	**4.** 41
5. 92	**6.** 98	**7.** 85	**8.** 52
9. 70	**10.** 42 + 28 = 70		

LESSON 43

ON YOUR OWN (PAGE 92): 29 − 13 = 16
PAGE 93

1. 24	**2.** 42	**3.** 33	**4.** 21
5. 25	**6.** 8	**7.** 10	**8.** 27
9. 25	**10.** 25 − 15 = 10		

LESSON 44

ON YOUR OWN (PAGE 95): 32 − 15 = 17
PAGE 96

1. 29	**2.** 48	**3.** 18	**4.** 28
5. 45	**6.** 9	**7.** 36	**8.** 27
9. 5	**10.** 32 − 24 = 8		

LESSON 45

ON YOUR OWN (PAGE 97): 31 − 13 = 18, 18 + 13 = 31
PAGE 98

1. 36, 36 + 8 = 44	**2.** 32, 32 + 7 = 39
3. 41, 41 + 5 = 46	**4.** 45, 45 + 13 = 58
5. 17, 17 + 26 = 43	**6.** 35, 35 + 49 = 84
7. 12, 12 + 17 = 29	**8.** 69, 69 + 23 = 92
9. 17, 17 + 57 = 74	**10.** 31, 31 + 28 = 59
11. 24, 24 + 20 = 44	**12.** 22, 22 + 38 = 60
13. 26 − 18 = 8	

LESSON 46

PAGE 100

1. 277	**2.** 186	**3.** 785	**4.** 218
5. 569	**6.** 568	**7.** 837	**8.** 535
9. 999	**10.** 425 + 320 = 745		

LESSON 47

ON YOUR OWN (PAGE 102): 439 + 276 = 715
PAGE 103

1. 381	**2.** 525	**3.** 337	**4.** 732
5. 399	**6.** 903	**7.** 257 + 306 = 563	

LESSON 48

PAGE 105

1. 412	**2.** 362	**3.** 540	**4.** 231
5. 316	**6.** 103	**7.** 671	**8.** 26
9. 110	**10.** 158 − 46 = 112		

LESSON 49

PAGE 108

1. 192	**2.** 708	**3.** 365	**4.** 179
5. 372	**6.** 346	**7.** 327 − 168 = 159	

LESSON 50

ON YOUR OWN (PAGE 110): 700 − 351 = 349
PAGE 111

1. 157	**2.** 428	**3.** 142	**4.** 294
5. 89	**6.** 306	**7.** 300 − 125 = 175	

LESSON 51

ON YOUR OWN (PAGE 112): 165, 773, 190, 963
PAGE 113

1. 85	**2.** 47	**3.** 16	**4.** 160
5. 645	**6.** 741	**7.** 841	**8.** 192
9. 624	**10.** 477	**11.** 473	**12.** 687
13. 449	**14.** 169	**15.** 278	**16.** 24
17. 245 + 629 = 874			